Macmillan Law Masters

Conveyancing

D0766713

Macmillan Law Masters

Series Editor: Marise Cremona

Business Law (2nd edn)   Stephen Judge
Company Law (3rd edn)   Janet Dine
Constitutional and Administrative Law (3rd edn)   John Alder
Contract Law (3rd edn)   Ewan McKendrick
Conveyancing (3rd edn)   Priscilla Sarton
Criminal Law (2nd edn)   Jonathan Herring and Marise Cremona
Employment Law (3rd edn)   Deborah J. Lockton
Environmental Law and Ethics   John Alder and David Wilkinson
Evidence   Raymond Emson
Family Law (2nd edn)   Kate Standley
Housing Law and Policy   David Cowan
Intellectual Property Law   Tina Hart and Linda Fazzani
Land Law (3rd edn)   Kate Green
Landlord and Tenant Law (3rd edn)   Margaret Wilkie and Godfrey Cole
Law of the European Union (2nd edn)   Jo Shaw
Law of Succession   Catherine Rendell
Law of Trusts   Patrick McLoughlin and Catherine Rendell
Legal Method (3rd edn)   Ian McLeod
Legal Theory   Ian McLeod
Social Security Law   Robert East
Torts (2nd edn)   Alastair Mullis and Ken Oliphant

Conveyancing

Priscilla Sarton
LL.M
Solicitor

Law series editor: Marise Cremona
Senior Fellow, Centre for Commercial Law Studies,
Queen Mary and Westfield College, University of London

Third Edition

First edition 1991
Reprinted 1992
Second edition 1993
Reprinted 1994
Third edition 2000
Published by
MACMILLAN PRESS LTD
Houndmills, Basingstoke, Hampshire RG21 6XS
and London
Companies and representatives throughout the world

ISBN 0–333–76080–8

A catalogue record for this book is available from the British Library.

This book is printed on paper suitable for recycling and made from
fully managed and sustained forest sources.

10   9   8   7   6   5   4   3   2   1
09   08 07 06 05 04 03 02 01 00

Printed in Great Britain by
Creative Print & Design (Wales), Ebbw Vale

Contents

Preface

It has been surprisingly difficult when writing this book to decide on the correct words to use. A professional conveyancer can be either female or male, and to add to the complexity of the matter, either a solicitor or a licensed conveyancer.

There has been no wish to imply that every legal adviser is a male solicitor, but the pressing need for brevity has meant that 'he' has had to be used for both sexes and 'solicitor' for both professions. It is hoped that readers will not take offence. Another difficulty has been the replacement of the traditional words 'vendor' and 'purchaser' by the modern 'seller' and 'buyer' in the new form of contract for sale. 'Seller' is used throughout this book, but the word 'purchaser' is not so easily displaced, as in the context of the Land Registration Act 1925, the Land Charges Act 1972 and other property legislation, 'purchaser' has a technical meaning that 'buyer' does not. The choice was either to use 'purchaser' in some chapters and 'buyer' in others, or stick consistently to 'purchaser'. The second course has been chosen.

The Law Society has helpfully given permission for the use of questions from its past examination papers. The answers are the author's, and are in no way connected with the Society. Thanks are due to the Law Society and the Solicitors' Law Stationery Society Ltd for their permission to reproduce the protocol documentation, including the form of contract for sale, and to the Law Society for its permission to quote from its 'Introduction to the Protocol'.

The book is dedicated to Mark Sarton, for without him it would never have been written, yet he has suffered so much through its writing.

PRISCILLA SARTON

Preface to the Third Edition

The only purpose of this preface is to re-dedicate the book to Mark Sarton, who read it and decided to become an anthropologist, and to thank firstly all the students who over the years have read it and kindly said they understood it and secondly Anne Ransome, Mavis Pearce and Evan Hughes for all their support in the 'day job'.

Table of Cases

Table of Statutes

Table of Statutory Instruments

1 Stages in a Residential Conveyancing Transaction from the Seller's Point of View

1.1 Introduction

This chapter introduces you to the steps taken on the sale of a freehold house. The sale of a leasehold property is dealt with in Chapter 16, and Chapter 13 deals with further points that have to be considered on the sale of commercial properties such as office premises.

In March 1990 the Law Society introduced the National Protocol for the sale of domestic freehold and leasehold property. The protocol sets out procedures which the Society recommends all solicitors to use. The purpose is to speed the transaction through, and particularly to reduce the time lag between the parties negotiating the sale and the formation of the formal and binding agreement to sell. Use of the protocol also involves the use of standardised documentation, namely a form of agreement for sale, property information forms and a 'fixtures, fittings and contents' form.

The protocol relates only to domestic transactions and even then it is not compulsory for a solicitor to use it, but its use is described by the Law Society as 'preferred practice'. It does anyway reflect procedures that are widespread. Every solicitor acting in a domestic transaction should notify the solicitor on the other side whether or not the protocol will be used. Once the protocol has been adopted for that transaction it must be followed, except that a solicitor may depart from it provided that he gives notice to the other side of his decision to do so. The protocol only governs procedures between the two solicitors. It does not affect matters between the solicitor and his client, or third parties such as mortgagees.

It is stressed again that a solicitor who uses the protocol might find himself doing little different from what he would have done anyway. The only departures from his previous practice might be the use of the standardised forms, and the amount of documentation (what the protocol calls 'the package') supplied to the purchaser's solicitor before the contract. Nor is the protocol designed to be an exhaustive list of steps to be taken, and the Law Society in its introduction to the protocol states that 'at all stages the solicitor's professional skills, knowledge and judgement will need to be applied in just the same way as it has been in the past'.

This chapter describes a protocol transaction, but also attempts to explain how the transaction would proceed if it were not governed by the protocol.

1.2 Your Client

Imagine that Robert Oates is planning to sell his present home. The house is freehold and is mortgaged to the Potteries Bank plc. He is also planning to instruct you to act for him. In what it calls the first step, the protocol suggests that Robert should call on you as soon as he decides to put his home on the market, so that you can immediately start to put together the pre-contract 'package'. You can send this without delay to the prospective purchaser as soon as he is found.

You probably have only a slender hope of Robert coming to you at this stage. The first person Robert will approach is the estate agent, and Robert will not approach you until the prospective purchaser is actually found. When this happens Robert will instruct you to act for him.

1.3 Gathering Information

(a) General

Your first task is to gather information. You need this in order to draft the agreement for sale. You also need it to complete the Seller's Property Information Form which you will be sending to the purchaser's solicitor. This form is in the Appendix to this book. Read it, and you will know the sort of information you need to collect.

This gathering of information is what the protocol calls 'preparing the package: assembling the information' (the 'package' being the documents that you will send as soon as possible to the purchaser's solicitor). It is nothing new; a seller's solicitor has always needed this information. The sources of information include your client, possibly the estate agent, and the documents of title. So imagine you have Robert sitting in your office.

(b) Interview with Client – Gathering Information about His Title

(i) You must ask your client where his title deeds or land certificate are as you need to investigate his title in order to draft the agreement for sale. The deeds might be in the possession of your client, but if the house is mortgaged, the lender will have them. Robert's deeds are with the Potteries Bank, his mortgagee. The Bank may, when it learns of the proposed sale, be prepared to instruct you to act for it in the redemption of the mortgage. It will then send you the original deeds or, in the case of registered title, the charge certificate. The Bank will expect an undertaking from you to the effect that you hold the deeds on its behalf, and if the sale falls through, will return the deeds in the same condition as they were when you received them.

If the Bank will not be instructing you, then it may be reluctant to let you have the originals. If the title is unregistered, the Bank will send you an abstract or epitome of the deeds.

If the title is registered, you only need the title number of the property. You can then obtain an office copy of the entries on the register and of the filed plan from the District Land Registry. If you do not know the title number, but are sure that the title is registered, you can apply for office copies without quoting the title number, as the Registry will obligingly look this up for you. It is always possible for you to discover whether or not a title is registered and its title number by making a search in the index map at the Registry. See Chapter 6, section 6.2(d).

(ii) Ask Robert if his neighbours have any sort of rights over his property, such as a right-of-way. The point is that easements do not always appear on the deeds or on the register of title. They may have arisen from long use. (If a house is one of a terrace there is often a right-of-way for each owner over the backyards of the houses, for access to a side entrance.) Similarly, does your client exercise rights over a neighbour's property? Does he obtain his gas, electricity, water, etc., directly from the public road, or across a neighbour's property?

If the last-mentioned, you have to find out if the pipes, etc., are there merely by the permission of the neighbour, or if Robert has easements over the neighbour's land (see question 5 on the property information form).

(iii) Does Robert live in the house with his wife? If so, is she a co-owner? Has she agreed to the sale? (If the answer to these questions is 'yes' you need instructions from her (see Chapter 11).

(iv) Could anyone else have a claim to own part of the house? For example, did anyone contribute to the original purchase price with the intention of owning a share? If the answer is 'yes', it will affect the provisions you put in the agreement for sale (see Chapter 11) and the answer to question 8 on the property information form.

(c) Interview with Client: Completing the Seller's Property Information Form

The property information form has to be completed partly by the seller and partly by you on the basis of information supplied by your client. You can go through the form with him now. Alternatively, you can give Robert the form to take away with him to complete at home.

(d) Interview with Client: Completing the Fixtures, Fittings and Contents Form

This form (which is part of the protocol documentation) lists most of the items likely to be found in an average house and about which there could possibly be an argument as to whether or not they are included in the sale. The items range from aerials to door-knockers. You may hand this form to Robert at the interview, but you will doubtless ask him to complete it at home. He will have to indicate which of the items are to be sold with the house.

(e)   Interview with Client: His Financial Position

What is your client's financial position? The mortgage to the Bank must be redeemed. The Bank should be asked for a redemption figure, on the basis that completion will take place in, say, six weeks time.

Ask Robert if there is a second mortgage. He may have borrowed money some time ago, signed a paper and not realised its significance.

If Robert's title is unregistered, a second mortgage may be revealed by a search against his name at the Land Charges Registry, where it would be registered as a CI or CIII land charge. If his title is registered, a search at HM District Land Registry may reveal a registered charge or an entry protecting an informal mortgage.

Robert, by virtue of an express or implied condition in the agreement for sale, will be promising that all mortgages will be redeemed. You need to check that the purchase price will be sufficient to discharge all the mortgages. If it is not, then he will have to find other funds with which to redeem them, or abandon the idea of selling the house. Usually, if your client is selling his house, he will be buying a new one. An example of the calculation of a client's financial position in such circumstances is given in Chapter 18.

(f)   Your Charges

Robert may ask you for an estimate of your charges for acting for him in the sale. You must calculate the disbursements that you will have to make, and your fees. You might wish to make it clear that you are giving an estimate only, and that you are not bound to the figure quoted. Nevertheless, any estimate must be realistic, based on a knowledge of the details of the transaction, and include all disbursements, e.g. stamp duty and VAT. No client will be favourably impressed if the quoted figure is greatly exceeded. If you offer a fixed charge, the prospective client should be told the length of time the offer will remain valid.

The Law Society recommends that any indication of charges should be either given, or confirmed, in writing.

1.4   Preparing the Package

If the seller's solicitor is following the protocol he must now assemble a package of documents to be sent to the purchaser's solicitor. For a freehold property this involves:

1.   Assembling evidence of the seller's title to the property. If his title is registered under the Land Registration Act 1925, the evidence will

consist of an office copy of the entries on the register of title, a copy of the filed plan and, possibly, copies of documents referred to on the register and details of overriding interests (see Chapter 3).

If the seller's title has not yet been registered, the seller's solicitor will have to prepare an epitome of title accompanied by photocopies of the relevant title deeds (see Chapter 8).

2. Drafting the agreement for sale.
3. If the title is unregistered, making a land charges search against the name of the seller and any previous estate owners whose names are not already covered by a satisfactory search certificate (see Chapters 4 and 9). The protocol requires this search to be done now as it is always sensible for a seller's solicitor to make it before drafting the agreement for sale, as without it he cannot be sure that he has full knowledge of his client's title (see Workshop section of Chapter 5).
4. If the title is unregistered, making an index map search to confirm that the title really is unregistered and is not affected by a caution against first registration.

The package sent to the purchaser on the sale of a freehold should include:

(a) two copies of the agreement for sale,
(b) the evidence of the seller's title,
(c) the Seller's Property Information Form,
(d) the completed Fixtures Fittings and Contents form,
(e) the results of any land charge search or of any index map search.

If the sale is of a leasehold house or flat, further documents should be added (see Chapter 16).

1.5 Drafting the Agreement for Sale

It would be a good idea to get the terminology correct before we go any further. 'Agreement for sale' is used to mean the document that embodies the contract. 'Contract' is used to mean the bargain that is contained in the agreement, and which will bind both parties. So when the parties enter into the agreement, they are bound by the contract set out in the agreement. This terminology echoes the definitions in condition 1 of the Standard Conditions of Sale.

When you have seen your client and obtained either the deeds or an up-to-date office copy of the entries on the register of title, you should be able to draft the agreement. The essential thing is that you do not allow your client to enter into a agreement which he has no hope of fulfilling. Remember that it is essential that you thoroughly investigate your client's title. Your investigation must be every bit as thorough as if you were buying, rather than selling, on his behalf. The agreement will contain express or implied promises as to the title, and if you find that your client cannot live up to these promises, because there is something wrong with his title, the promises must be altered.

The agreement is prepared in duplicate. Both copies (or, as they are often called, 'parts') are sent to the purchaser's solicitor for approval. He will return one copy either unaltered or with amendments.

When the terms of the agreement are finally approved on behalf of both parties, one part of the agreement will be signed by the seller and one by the purchaser. The signature will usually be that of the client, not the solicitor. It is not usually part of the solicitor's authority actually to sign the agreement. So, if you find that the agreement has been signed by the purchaser's solicitor, you must ask him for evidence that his client has authorised him to do this.

The reason why the agreement is prepared in duplicate is that the parties intend to exchange the two parts. The seller will then have the part signed by the purchaser, and the purchaser will have the part signed by the seller. As exchange is contemplated by both parties, the contract will not come into existence until exchange takes place. Once exchange has taken place, the parties are contractually bound to one another.

1.6   Exchanging the Two Parts of the Agreement

Once the purchaser's solicitor is satisfied that the results of all the pre-contract searches and enquiries are satisfactory and that his client can safely enter into the contract, exchange will take place. Once the two parts of the agreement have been exchanged, the parties are bound: the seller to transfer ownership, and the purchaser to pay the purchase price.

(a)   Personal Exchange

This is where the seller's solicitor meets the purchaser's solicitor and the two parts of the agreement are exchanged. This method of exchange is rare because a solicitor cannot usually spare the time involved in travelling to a colleague's office.

(b)   Exchange through the Post

The purchaser's solicitor posts his client's part of the agreement to the seller's solicitor, together with the solicitor's cheque for the deposit. When the seller's solicitor receives these, he posts the part of the agreement signed by the seller back to the purchaser's solicitor.

Despite the long use of this method of exchange, there is still controversy as to the exact moment that the exchange takes place. One view is that exchange has occurred (and that the contract therefore exists) as soon as the second part of the agreement is put in the post. The other view is that exchange has not taken place until the second part of the agreement is actually received by the addressee. If the agreement incorporates the standard conditions (see Chapter 5) the contract will provide that exchange is to be treated as taking place on the *posting* of the second part, not on its receipt. (See standard condition 2.1.1.) If Robert is not buying a new house, this method of exchange would be satisfactory. If he is buying a new house, the exchange of agreements on his sale needs to be synchronised with the exchange of agreements on his purchase, and this is not easily done if the agreements are exchanged by post.

(c)   Exchange by Telephone

In this case, exchange takes place by it being agreed over the telephone that the two parts of the agreement are to be *treated* as exchanged.

Suppose that this method of exchange is contemplated on Robert's sale. The purchaser's solicitor might send his part of the agreement, together with a cheque for the deposit, to you. The accompanying letter is likely to say that these are not sent by way of exchange, but that you are to hold them to the order of the purchaser. This means that you cannot foist an exchange on the purchaser by posting the part of the agreement signed by Robert. Exchange cannot take place until the purchaser is ready. When the purchaser is ready, his solicitor will telephone you, and say that he is ready to exchange contracts. It will then be agreed on the telephone that contracts are now exchanged. You, as Robert's solicitor, will agree that you now hold his part of the agreement to the order of the purchaser, and that you will post it that day.

It is possible to agree exchange over the telephone before either seller or purchaser has parted with his part of the contract. In such a case, the purchaser's solicitor will give an undertaking to post his client's part of the contract and deposit cheque that day, and you will undertake to post Robert's part of the contract.

You can see that although the exchange takes place when that is agreed on the telephone, this is always followed (or possibly preceded) by the exchange of the documents themselves.

The drawback to this method of exchange is that it has taken place through a conversation, which might later be denied. For this reason, the Law Society recommends that written notes be taken by both parties as to what was said. It also recommends that the solicitors should agree that the telephone exchange be governed by either Law Society formula A (to be used where the purchaser has already sent a signed agreement to the seller's solicitor) or formula B (to be used when each solicitor still holds his own client's part of the agreement).

Both formulae provide for the insertion in the agreement of an agreed completion date, for confirmation that both parts of the agreement include any negotiated amendments, and for the giving of the undertakings outlined above.

(An attempt to explain Law Society formula C is made in Chapter 18.)

Warning **Whatever method of exchange is used, exchange will not be treated as having taken place unless the contents of the two parts of the agreement are identical. This is why it is essential that any alteration to the draft agreement is written into *both* parts before they are exchanged. It is salutory to read the case of *Harrison v. Battye* [1974].**

1.7   The Deposit

On exchange, the purchaser will normally have to pay a deposit of 10 per cent of the purchase price (see Chapter 5). This is part-payment of the purchase price, but it is also something more. It is a pledge of the purchaser's intention to fulfil the contract. If the purchaser unjustifiably refuses to complete, the deposit is forfeited to the seller.

If the contract provides for payment of a deposit, and the purchaser fails to do this (either because no payment is ever made, or because his cheque is dishonoured) the purchaser is considered to have broken the contract in such a fundamental way as to enable the seller to treat the contract as discharged (see standard condition 2.2.4). The seller is released from the contract, and can also sue for the unpaid deposit (see *Damon Cia Naviera SA v. Hapag-Lloyd International SA* [1985]).

1.8   Insurance

If nothing is said to the contrary in the contract, the risk of capital loss passes to the purchaser as soon as the two parts of the agreement are exchanged. So if, for example, the house burns down, the purchaser bears the loss and remains liable for the full purchase price. Two things might mitigate his loss:

1. after exchange the seller owes the purchaser a duty to take reasonable care of the property until completion of the sale. So if the fire could be traced back to the negligence of the seller, he would be liable to compensate the purchaser;
2. if the seller had maintained his own insurance on the house (which is likely, although he is under no duty to the purchaser to do so), then the insurance money due under the policy is held by the seller on trust for the purchaser. (This is the effect of s.47 of the Law of Property Act 1925.)

If the contract incorporates the standard conditions of sale (see Chapter 5) standard condition 5.1 alters these rules entirely. In Condition 5.1.1 the seller promises the purchaser to transfer the property in the same physical state as it was at the date of the contract (with the exception of fair wear and tear, i.e. ordinary dilapidation). This means that the risk of physical damage remains with the seller. It is therefore essential for the seller to continue to insure the property until the sale is completed, for his own protection. (Condition 5.3 makes it clear that the seller does not owe a duty to the purchaser to insure the property, and s.47 of the Law of the Property Act 1925 is excluded.)

So, if for example, the house burns down before completion, or is in any way physically damaged, the seller must compensate the purchaser, which will amount to the purchaser paying a reduced purchase price.

Condition 5.1.2 creates rights to rescind the contract, i.e. set it aside as if it had never existed. It applies when, before completion, the change in the physical state of the property makes the property unusable for its purpose at the date of the contract. In these circumstances the purchaser can rescind the contract, i.e. he does not merely pay a reduced price; he need not buy the property at all, unless he wishes.

In the same circumstances, a right of rescission is also given to the seller, but in his case only if the damage is of a sort that he could not reasonably have insured against, or if it is damage that it is not legally possible for him to make good. For instance, this could be because he could not get planning permission. Why should a seller wish to rescind if the property is severely damaged? Presumably because faced with a greatly reduced purchase price, he prefers not to sell at all, perhaps because it will leave him without enough money to buy a new house. (Remember that the seller has the right of rescission if he *could not* insure; not because he *did not* insure.)

Condition 5.1 applies only to an alteration in the physical state of the property, but this is not the only thing that can decrease its value. For example the fact that the property is listed as being of exceptional historical or architectural merit can remove any development value from the land. The risk of this sort of capital loss continues to pass to the purchaser on exchange of agreements.

Despite Condition 5.1 some purchasers will still prefer to insure the property themselves as from the date of the contract, preferring to have a claim against an insurance company rather than against the seller. If a purchaser does this the property will be doubly insured, i.e. by both seller and purchaser. The effect of double insurance is that each insurance company will pay only part of the claim, so the seller may find that his insurance company will pay only, say, half the loss, leaving the other half to be paid by the purchaser's insurer. The seller should consider putting into the contract a condition saying that if the seller's payment from the insurance company is reduced for this reason, then the compensation to be paid by him to the purchaser will be reduced by the same amount. The purchaser will recoup himself from the proceeds of his own policy.

Note: the position as to risk and insurance changes if the purchaser is allowed to occupy the house before completion – see standard conditions 5.2.3 and 5.2.2.

1.9   Proving Title

If the seller's solicitor is following the protocol, the package of documents sent to the purchaser's solicitor before the agreement is made will include evidence of the seller's title. The seller is said to have 'deduced' his title.

Usually, the purchaser's solicitor will consider this evidence when he receives the package, and so before his client enters into the agreement to buy. However it is, at least in theory, possible for the purchaser to investigate title after entering into the agreement. Why? It is because the agreement will contain a promise (usually implied rather than expressed) by the seller that he has a good title to the property. If the purchaser does not investigate title until after he has entered into the agreement, he is relying on this promise. If his subsequent investigation of title reveals that there is a defect in the seller's title that he was not told about at the time of the agreement he can say that the defect is a breach of contract, and possibly that the contract is discharged by breach. The purchaser is then released from his obligation to buy.

Of course there is considerable inconvenience for a purchaser in this position, who is probably committed to an agreement to sell his existing house and so you may be asking yourself 'why does a purchaser not always investigate title *before* he agrees to buy?' Well, invariably a purchaser does, for the practical reason mentioned above. Whether he *has* to depends on the terms of the contract.

If the purchaser is entitled to raise requisitions on the title (i.e. object that the title is not as promised in the contract) after exchange, he can leave investigation of title until then if he wishes to do so. This is the position envisaged by the standard conditions of sale (see Chapter 5). If a special condition in the contract precludes the purchaser from raising requisitions after exchange, the purchaser *must* investigate title before contract, as it will generally be too late to object to the title after the contract is made.

Chapter 5 explains the promises as to title given by the seller and Chapters 7 and 8 explain the evidence of title that the seller must supply.

1.10   Dealing with the Purchaser's Requisitions on Title

If the purchaser is dissatisfied either with the soundness of the title or with the evidence of the title that is given, he will 'raise a requisition on title'. In other words, he will complain to you about what is wrong and ask you to put it right. When faced with the purchaser's complaint, the seller may be able to put the matter right. He may, for example, be able to supply a missing document, or prove that a third-party interest is no longer enforceable against the land.

If the seller cannot put the matter right, his position depends on whether the purchaser is investigating title before or after exchange. If the former, the purchaser will not enter into agreement. If the purchaser is investigating title after exchange, then generally the seller must face the fact that he is in breach of his contract. He cannot live up to his promise as to title. He awaits the purchaser's decision. The purchaser may be able to treat the contract as discharged by the breach, and cease to be under any obligation to buy. He may also be able to sue for damages. The damages may be heavy.

It is unfortunately true that the fact that your client is in breach of contract *may* be your fault. Why did you not notice that his title was defective when you investigated it prior to drafting the agreement for sale? You could then, by a special condition in the agreement, have disclosed the defect and prevented the purchaser from raising the requisition (turn to Chapter 5).

1.11 Checking the Draft Conveyance or Transfer

Assuming that you are able to deal with any requisition, you now read the draft conveyance or transfer. This is drawn up by the purchaser's solicitor, but has to be approved by the seller's solicitor, who must check that it is not drawn so as to give the purchaser more than the seller contracted to give.

Once the draft has been approved by you, the purchaser's solicitor will 'engross' it, i.e. prepare a fair copy of it. This will be sent to you so that you can arrange to have it executed by your client.

1.12 Completion Statement

When you send to the purchaser's solicitor your replies to his requisitions on title, and the approved draft transfer, you will also send him a completion statement, setting out the sum that the purchaser must pay on completion. This may consist merely of the purchase price, less the deposit already paid. There may sometimes be other items, for example:

(a) *apportionments of outgoings.* At one time it was usual to apportion the water and sewage charges, gas and electricity bills, so that if the seller had paid for a period extending beyond the completion date, he was credited with an apportioned part of the payment. This is not now usually done. The seller usually tells the relevant authorities of his date of departure and ensures that the meters are read as close as possible to the date of completion. He is then sent bills from the bodies concerned. The purchaser is responsible for the charges arising from the date of completion.

An apportionment is still usual in an assignment of a lease. The rent might have to be apportioned, and so might payments made to the landlord in respect of insurance or maintenance.

(b) *interest*. If completion takes place later than the date agreed in the contract, either seller or purchaser might be liable to pay interest on the unpaid balance of the purchase price. The amount involved will be deducted from, or added to, the purchase price (see Chapter 19).

1.13   Completion

Completion at its simplest is a swop. The purchaser pays the balance of the purchase price in return (in the case of an unregistered title) for the deeds and the conveyance to him. The purchaser will then own the legal estate and the beneficial interest. If the seller's title is registered, the purchaser will receive the land certificate and the transfer. He will then own the beneficial interest, but will not own the legal estate until he is registered as the new proprietor (see Chapter 3). In our case, Robert's title is mortgaged. The purchaser will want evidence that the mortgage has been paid off. In unregistered title, he will demand that a receipt be endorsed on the mortgage deed, and executed by the mortgagee. In registered title, he will be given the charge certificate (or charge certificates, if there is more than one registered charge) and a form DS1 for each charge. This is discussed further in Chapters 7 and 9.

1.14   After Completion

(a) You should now account to Robert for the proceeds of sale. You will usually have secured your client's authority to deduct from them your fees and disbursements, and any fees due to the estate agent. The balance, with a statement showing clearly how the balance is arrived at, is remitted according to your client's instructions.
(b) Any undertakings that have been given to the purchaser's solicitor must be complied with, e.g. in connection with the redemption of your client's mortgage.

2 Stages in a Conveyancing Transaction: The Purchaser's Point of View

2.1 Introduction

This chapter takes you through a transaction again, but this time from a purchaser's point of view. Imagine that you are acting for Susan Holt in her purchase of a house. She has applied for a mortgage loan from a building society, and you find that the society is prepared to instruct you to act for it in the creation of the mortgage. You have, therefore, two clients (see section 2.18 on conflict of interest).

2.2 Gathering Information

(a) Susan must give you details of the bargain that has been struck so that you can judge if the draft agreement prepared by the seller represents that bargain. Were fittings included in the sale, and at what price? What sort of completion date has been arranged between the parties?

(b) Was there anything about the property that struck her? Did anyone appear to have any sort of access over the property? Who appeared to be living on the property apart from the seller?

2.3 You Need to Know your Client's Financial Position

(a) Total Purchase Price

The first point is that you must make sure that she realises the *total* cost of the purchase. This may well take her by surprise. She needs an estimate of your fees and details of your foreseeable disbursements. These will include stamp duty (see 2.17) and Land Registry fees.

(b) Mortgage Offer

The second point is that as she is buying with the aid of a mortgage loan, you must be sure that the lender has made a *formal* offer of a loan before you commit your client to the agreement to buy.

When you read the formal offer, check the amount of the loan. Is this the amount your client expects? Is there any retention clause (see Chapter 18). Is there any condition that must be satisfied before the loan is made? (An example might be that the Society wants a specialist survey done on some part of the house, e.g. for risk of subsidence. The money will only be available when the survey is done, and if the Society considers the result to be satisfactory.) If the mortgage is an endowment mortgage, the offer will be conditional on the life policy being on foot before completion. The proposal form for the assurance should be completed now and forwarded either to the lender or the assurance company, and confirmation that the proposal has been accepted by the company is needed *before contract.*

(c)   Deposit

A contract usually provides for a deposit of 10 per cent of the purchase price to be paid on exchange of contracts. Your client must realise that this may be forfeited to the seller if it is your client's fault that completion does not take place. So any failure by her to complete will involve her in severe financial loss, even if the seller is in fact able to sell the house to someone else at the same, or even an increased, price. Of course, if the failure to complete is the seller's fault, Susan will be entitled to the return of the deposit.

If Susan does not have enough money to pay a 10 per cent deposit on exchange of contracts, there are various solutions:

(i) If she is selling her existing house to buy the new one, she will be receiving a deposit from her purchaser, and this may be used to finance the deposit which she has to pay to her seller (see Chapter 5 for details on the drafting of the contract for sale). However, if she is trading up – e.g. selling an £80 000 house and buying a new one for £120 000, she will still have to find £4000.

(ii) She may be able to persuade the seller to accept a smaller deposit, e.g. on the above example £8000 rather than £12 000. The seller may be unhappy with this, as he knows that if she fails to complete she will be forfeiting to him a significantly smaller sum.

However, he may be comforted by Standard Condition 6.8.4. This gives a seller who accepts less than the 10 per cent deposit a right to sue for the balance if he is forced to serve a completion notice because of the purchaser's delay in completion. So if things go wrong, the seller may be able to recover the missing £4000, always provided, of course, that Susan is not insolvent.

(iii) She may have to borrow the deposit, the loan either to be repaid when the mortgage loan is forthcoming at completion, or to be added to the mortgage debt. The customer's bank is a traditional source for such a loan, but building societies now have the power to lend on unsecured loans, as well as secured ones, so the building society may provide the deposit at exchange of contracts, instead of withholding the entire advance until completion. The mortgage, when made, will then charge the land with repayment of the total loan, including the amount lent to fund the deposit;

(iv) She may be able to use a deposit insurance scheme. The idea is that an insurance company, in return for a one-off premium (to be paid by the purchaser), promises the seller that if the contract is not performed owing to the purchaser's default, the company will pay the seller the 10 per cent deposit. It usually costs less to pay the premium than to pay the interest on a loan for the deposit.

2.4 The Pre-contract Searches and Enquiries

As you will see in Chapter 5 the seller has a limited duty to tell the purchaser about defects in his title to the property and about third-party rights over it, such as restrictive covenants or easements. The duty stops there. So there is a great deal of information which might well affect the purchaser's decision as to whether or not to buy the property and which she must find out for herself, and she must do this *before* she enters into the agreement to buy. To take a simple example, the seller may know that the Motorway M1001 is to be built on the far side of the garden fence. The purchaser, however, does not learn this interesting fact until after she has agreed to buy the house. It is too late. The seller was under no duty to inform the purchaser about the proposed motorway. He has not broken a term of the contract, so the purchaser must either complete or lose her deposit and face a claim for damages. This is why it is so important for the purchaser to make enquiries about the property *before* contract.

Pre-contract searches and enquiries are dealt with in Chapter 6.

2.5 Consideration of the Draft Agreement

Once the draft agreement has been received in duplicate from the seller, you must consider if it represents the bargain that your client expects. If there is any doubt, Susan must again be consulted. She should also be asked on what date she wishes to complete as the completion date will be put in the agreement on exchange.

2.6 The Deposit

The deposit payable on exchange must now be obtained from the client. (The need to provide this deposit has already been discussed with her.) If your client is to give you a cheque, you should receive it sufficiently early for the cheque to be cleared before you draw on it to pay the seller. According to standard condition 2.2.1 (see Chapter 5) the deposit should be paid to the seller by banker's draft or by a cheque drawn on a solicitor's bank account. This, if complied with, should remove any possibility that the cheque will bounce. Condition 2.2.4 provides that if any cheque for the deposit is dishonoured, the seller can treat the contract as discharged.

2.7   Exchange of the Two Parts of the Agreement

Once you are satisfied:

(a) that the purchaser will have the necessary funds on completion to buy the property and to pay all attendant expenses;
(b) that the replies to all the pre-contract searches and enquiries are satisfactory;
(c) that the draft agreement is satisfactory;
(d) if it is to be investigated before exchange, that the title is satisfactory;

you may exchange agreements on behalf of your client. On exchange, a date for completion, previously settled between the parties, will be put in both parts of the agreement.

2.8   Insurance

We have seen that if the contract incorporates the standard conditions, the risk of physical damage to the property no longer passes to the purchaser on exchange of agreement. It is therefore not essential for a purchaser to insure against that risk until completion. However, as Susan is buying with the aid of a mortgage loan, you must check the *lender's* requirements as to insurance. The lender may require the borrower to take out comprehensive insurance as from the time the money is made available, which may be earlier than actual completion.

2.9   Investigation of Title

Once the contract is made, the purchaser will investigate title (see Chapters 7 and 9) and may raise requisitions on title. (Remember, though, what was said in Chapter 1, section 10. If the agreement by a special condition, prevents the purchaser from raising requisitions after contract, the purchaser *must* investigate title before exchange.)

The contract will, through the general conditions, provide a timetable for the stages of the transaction. Standard condition 4 says that requisitions must be raised within six working days of receipt of the seller's evidence of title, or if this was provided before exchange, within six days of the exchange. The purchaser must be careful to observe this particular time limit as the condition provides that the purchaser's right to raise requisitions is lost after the six days have passed. In other words, if the purchaser does not object to the title *within* the time limits, she may be unable to object at all, and will have to accept the title with its defects. This condition will not prevent requisitions being raised out of time in some circumstances. A requisition can be raised out of time if it is as to a defect that is only revealed when the original title deeds themselves are seen, which may not be until completion. An example would be a memorandum of severance endorsed on a conveyance to joint tenants (see Chapter 11) if the abstract of title did not disclose the existence of this memorandum. Another exception is where the pre-completion search reveals a defect which was not disclosed by the abstract of title. Again, a requisition can be raised out of time.

The purchaser's solicitor must also remember that there is a time limit in standard condition 4 for the purchaser to raise observations on the seller's replies to the requisitions, and that this limit must be strictly observed.

2.10   Report on Title to the Building Society

You are investigating title not only on behalf of Susan Holt, but also on behalf of her mortgagee. Once you are satisfied that the title, and the evidence of the title, are satisfactory, you will report to that effect to the Building Society.

You might, however, have found a defect in title, and one that you consider to be sufficiently serious to affect the value of the property. Susan, because she likes the house so much, might be willing to press ahead. You owe a duty to the Building Society. You must report on the defect to the Society, with the possible result that the offer of the mortgage will be withdrawn. (This should not leave Susan Holt stranded, as if the defect is sufficiently serious to lead to the withdrawal of the mortgage offer, it will probably be a ground for Susan treating the contract to buy as discharged by the seller's breach.)

If Susan Holt will not consent to your informing the Society, you will have to tell the Society you can no longer act for it. The Society will instruct another solicitor, who will investigate title and discover the defect. So Susan might as well accept the inevitable.

2.11   Drafting the Conveyance or Transfer

It is your task to draft the purchase deed, and two copies of your draft will be sent, with your requisitions on title, to the seller's solicitor. Drafting is discussed in Chapters 14 and 15.

The seller's solicitor will return one copy of the draft, either approved or amended. Once any amendments have been negotiated and agreed, you will have the deed engrossed. You must then consider whether or not it is necessary for your client to execute it. It is often unnecessary for the purchaser to execute the deed, but she should do so if the deed contains covenants given to the seller. The deed should also be executed by co-purchasers, if it contains a declaration as to how they own the beneficial interest, i.e. whether as joint tenants or in shares. Execution of the deed makes this declaration binding upon them.

The deed is then sent to the seller's solicitor for execution by his client. The deed will then be retained by the seller's solicitor until completion.

2.12 Drafting the Mortgage

Your client will have a choice of mortgage. There are two main types, the repayment mortgage, and the interest-only mortgage.

Under the repayment mortgage, the borrower promises monthly payments of capital and interest over a period of years. The maximum is usually 40 years. The capital debt is therefore slowly reduced. If the borrower expects to be survived by a spouse or by dependants for whom a home must be provided, he would be well advised to take out a mortgage protection policy. If the borrower dies before the mortgage loan is repaid, the policy will provide the money to pay off the balance due.

In the case of an interest-only mortgage, during the term of the mortgage the borrower pays only the interest. He plans to repay the capital in a lump sum at the end of the term. The lender will want to be satisfied that the borrower has made some sort of arrangement to raise the necessary sum.

The classic interest-only mortgage is the endowment mortgage. The borrower takes out an assurance policy on his life. The policy will mature (i.e. pay out) at the end of the mortgage term. The policy promises a fixed minimum sum if it matures at the end of the mortgage term. In addition, the assurance company declares annual bonuses which are added to the fixed sum, and a terminal bonus at the end of the term. The monthly premiums are calculated in the expectation that the fixed sum and the bonuses will together yield at least enough to repay the mortgage loan.

The policy will also mature if the borrower dies before the end of the mortgage term. If this is what happens, the policy promises sufficient money to repay the entire mortgage loan. There is therefore no need for the borrower to take out a mortgage protection policy.

The policy is either formally assigned to the lender, or is deposited with him.

The endowment mortgage is falling out of favour. The size of the bonuses depends on the success of the assurance company's investments, and therefore the performance of companies' shares on the stock exchange. In recent years, some borrowers have had the unpleasant experience of receiving a letter from the assurance company telling them that the money yielded by the policy was unlikely to be enough to pay off the mortgage.

An additional problem is that any sort of life assurance must be looked upon as a long-term investment. A borrower who attempts to surrender a policy in its early years (i.e. asks the assurance company to end the contract and to pay out early) will receive back from the company less, or little more, than he has paid in premiums. Even a surrender in later years will be disadvantageous, as the borrower will not receive the terminal bonus, which is often a large part of the final payment. In fact, it is often more profitable to sell an endowment policy than to surrender it.

The fact that an endowment policy is such a long-term investment does not matter if the borrower wants to sell his house to buy another, as the same policy will be used as security for the repayment of the new loan, and will not be surrendered. It is a disadvantage if the borrower, perhaps because of financial difficulties or marriage, wishes to sell his house and not buy another. He is left with a policy on which he must pay premiums for several years if he wants anything like a real return on his investment.

An alternative to an endowment mortgage is a mortgage which depends on a portfolio of stock exchange investments to yield the capital sum. This has sometimes taken the form of a PEPS mortgage, where a 'personal equity plan' has been relied upon to provide the redemption money. Another scheme is to rely on a retirement plan to yield on retirement a lump sum sufficient to pay off the mortgage.

Which sort of mortgage is best for your client depends on his financial and family circumstances. You must realise that your client is coming to you from the estate agent who has probably arranged the mortgage finance and possibly a life policy. Many estate agents are now owned by insurance companies, building societies or banks, and so may not, or perhaps cannot (because of the Financial Services Act 1986) give a choice of lender or assurance policy to the customer. Consider the suitability of the financial package that has been arranged, and whether a straight repayment mortgage might not be more suitable for your client than an endowment mortgage (see Chapter 25, para. 25.09 of the Law Society's Guide to the Professional Conduct of Solicitors, 7th Edition).

As, in this case, you are also the solicitor for the Building Society, it will be your task to draft the mortgage documents. The Society will send you its standard form of mortgage, and you will only have to fill in the blanks with details of the property, the borrower, amount of loan, etc. In the case of an endowment mortgage you may have to prepare the deed of assignment of the assurance policy. (The policy will, of course, be reassigned when the loan is repaid.) It may also be necessary after completion to give notice to the assurance company that the policy has been assigned. This is important for two reasons. It ensures that when the policy monies are payable they will be paid to the Building Society rather than to Susan. It also preserves the priority of the mortgage, and prevents a later mortgagee of the policy gaining priority over the Society's mortgage. Two copies of the notice are prepared. After completion, both copies are sent to the assurance company which is asked to receipt one copy of the notice and return it. This is then carefully preserved for fear the company might one day deny having been given notice. (Increasingly, lenders do not ask the borrower actually to assign the policy, but only *to promise* to assign it if required to do so. Nor is any notice of the assignment given to the assurance company. This is because it is likely that the house will be sold before the policy matures, and the loan repaid from the sale proceeds rather than the policy proceeds.)

Susan will have to execute the mortgage and the assignment of the policy as well as, possibly, the conveyance or transfer (see earlier). Your instructions from the Building Society may tell you to ensure that the mortgage documents are signed in the presence of a solicitor, or legal executive, or licenced conveyancer. This will mean that she will have to come into your office. So ensure that she has had your completion statement (see Chapter 2, section 13) and can bring the balance of the purchase price with her when she comes, and be sure that the appointment leaves time for any personal cheque of hers to be cleared before completion.

2.13   Obtaining the Balance of the Purchase Money

(a) From the Building Society. When you reported to the Society that the title was in order, you would also have asked them to send you the advance in time for completion.
(b) From your client. You need to send a statement to Susan, setting out the sum needed from her to complete the purchase. It will consist of the purchase price (less the deposit paid on contract) plus any apportionment of outgoings, plus your fees for acting in the purchase and in the mortgage, plus all the disbursements, minus the net mortgage loan.

2.14   The Pre-completion Search

Shortly before completion, you must make the pre-completion search. This really represents the final step in the investigation of the seller's title.

Completion must not take place until the results of the search are known, and must then take place before the priority period given by the official search certificate expires.

If you are buying a registered title, the search is made at the appropriate District Land Registry. If you are buying an unregistered title, the search is made at the Land Charges Registry at Plymouth (see Chapters 7 and 9 for a further explanation of these searches).

2.15   Completion

On completion you will pay the balance of the purchase price to the seller's solicitor. This will usually be paid by banker's draft or it may be telegraphed directly to the bank account of the seller's solicitor.

You will expect to pick up:

(a) if the title is unregistered, the deeds and the conveyance to Susan executed by the seller. If the seller had a mortgage, the purchaser is entitled to see that this is discharged. The mortgage deed itself will be handed over, properly receipted by the lender, or instead the solicitor acting for the mortgagee (who will probably be the same solicitor as is acting for the seller) will give you 'the usual undertakings' (these are explained in Chapter 7);

(b) In registered conveyancing, the land certificate and the transfer executed by the seller. If the seller had a mortgage, you will pick up the charge certificate, the transfer, and Land Registry Form DSI (the recent replacement for Land Registry Form 53), or the usual undertakings in respect of it (see Chapter 7).

If the parties' solicitors are actually going to attend completion, it will usually take place at the offices of the seller's solicitor. (On this point, see standard condition 6.2.) (If this involves a long journey for the purchaser's solicitor, he can instruct another solicitor to act as his agent.) These civilised meetings are becoming things of the past, and completion increasingly takes place through the post. The purchaser's solicitor telegraphs the purchase price to the seller's solicitor, and in return the seller's solicitor posts the deeds to the purchaser's solicitor. Certain tasks have to be undertaken by the seller's solicitor as agent for the purchaser's solicitor, e.g. the examination and marking of the deeds, and endorsement of memoranda. An important point for the purchaser's solicitor to have confirmed is that the seller's solicitor has authority from the seller's mortgagee to receive the money to be used to redeem the mortgage. Otherwise, if the seller's solicitor disappears with the money, the seller's mortgagee can refuse to discharge the mortgage (see *Edward Wong Finance Co. Ltd* v. *Johnson Stokes and Master [1984]*).

The Law Society has published a code for postal completions, designed to define the solicitors' responsibilities and to reduce risk. If the solicitors are following the protocol, they must agree to adhere to the code, but otherwise do not have to do so.

2.16 After Completion

(a) You must report to your client that completion has taken place and that she can now move in. Keys are usually left with the estate agents, rather than with the solicitors.

(b) You can now transfer the sums paid to you by Susan Holt in respect of your fees and disbursements from your clients' account to your office account.

(c) If your client has bought the property subject to a lease, the tenant should be given written notice of the identity of his new landlord. If you fail to give this notice to a residential tenant, any rent or service charge due from him will be treated as not being due, and so no action for non-payment can be taken (section 48 of the Landlord & Tenant Act 1987).

(d) Perfecting the title. As purchaser's solicitor, ask yourself two questions:

  (i) does the conveyance or transfer need stamping with *ad valorem* stamp duty, and/or the 'particulars delivered' stamp?

  (ii) is the purchaser affected by the Land Registration Act 1925?

If you have bought an unregistered title, you need to consider whether or not you must apply for first registration of your client's title (see Chapter 3). You have two months in which to apply. You will be applying for registration of Susan as proprietor, and also for registration of the Society's mortgage.

If you have bought a registered title, you must apply for registration of the transfer to your client. Only when registered will your client obtain the legal estate. The application for registration should be made before the priority period given by the pre-completion search expires (see Chapter 7). You will also be applying for registration of the Society's mortgage as a registered charge.

2.17 A Note on the Stamping of Documents by the Purchaser after Completion

(a) Rates of Duty

  (i) *Ad valorem* and fixed-rate stamp duty.

  A conveyance or transfer on sale of a freehold or an existing leasehold estate is liable to *ad valorem* stamp duty at the rate of 3.5 per cent of the consideration paid. If the transfer contains a certificate that the consideration (i.e. the purchase price) does not exceed £500 000, the rate is 2.5 per cent.

  If it contains a certificate that the consideration does not exceed £250 000, the rate is 1 per cent.

  If it contains a certificate that the consideration does not exceed £60 000, the transfer is exempt from duty. (For full wording of this certificate, see the conveyance in Chapter 14.)

 (ii) Stamp duty does not have to be paid on mortgages or vacating receipts executed after 1971.

(iii) A conveyance or transfer by way of gift executed after 30 April 1987 is exempt from stamp duty, provided it contains a certificate that it is an instrument within one of the categories of exempt documents under Stamp Duty (Exempt Instruments) Regulations 1987 (SI 1987/516).

(iv) An assent executed as a deed, an appointment of a new trustee, a conveyance or transfer in consideration of marriage, or as part of rearrangement of property on a divorce are now exempt from the 50p deed stamp, provided they are certified as in paragraph (iii) above.

(v) A power of attorney is not liable for stamp duty (s.85 of the Finance Act 1985).

(vi) An assent not executed as a deed is not liable for stamp duty.

(b) Time Limit for Stamping

The conveyance or other document should be presented for stamping within thirty days of its execution. The date of execution is taken as the date which the conveyance bears (i.e. usually the date of completion). There are financial penalties (which can be severe) if a document is presented for stamping after the thirty-day period, and the Land Registry will not register any conveyance or transfer that is not properly stamped.

(c) 'Particulars Delivered' Stamp

The Finance Act 1931 provides that certain documents must be produced to the Inland Revenue, together with a form giving particulars of the documents and any consideration received. The form is kept by the Inland Revenue (it provides useful information for the assessment of the value of the land) and the document is stamped with a stamp (generally called the PD stamp) as proof of its production. Without this PD stamp the document is not properly stamped and the person who failed in his responsibility to produce it (i.e. the original purchaser) can be fined.

The documents that need a PD stamp are:

(i) a conveyance on sale of the freehold;
(ii) a grant of a lease for seven years or more;
(iii) the transfer on sale of a lease of seven years or more.

If a conveyance or transfer is being sent to the Land Registry for registration, and it is not liable for *ad valorem* stamp duty but does need a PD stamp (i.e. the sale was for £60000 or less and the document contains the necessary certificate) the document need not be produced at the Inland Revenue before the application for registration is made. Instead, the form giving particulars is sent with the application for registration to the Land Registry, which forwards the form to the Inland Revenue.

2.18 Acting for Both Parties

We have treated acting for the seller and acting for the purchaser as alternatives. Is it possible for a solicitor to act for both?

The usual answer is 'no' because Rule 6 of the Law Society Practice Rules 1990 forbids it. Similarly, the same solicitor (or two or more solicitors acting in partnership or association) cannot act for both landlord and tenant. However, Rule 6 does permit a solicitor to act for both parties in a very limited number of cases. Even in one of these cases, a solicitor cannot act for both parties unless both parties consent, there is no conflict of interest between them, and the seller is not selling as a builder. For full details of Rule 6 see Chapter 25 para. 25.01 of the Law Society's Guide to the Professional Conduct of Solicitors, 7th Edition.

A conflict of interest may become apparent to you when you are drafting the contract for sale. As soon as you find yourself putting in a special condition that is to the disadvantage of the purchaser, e.g. cutting down his power of investigating title or preventing him from objecting to a defect in title, you should realise that you cannot also advise the purchaser on the wisdom of accepting the condition.

There is no rule of professional conduct to prevent a solicitor acting for co-sellers, or for co-purchasers unless there is a conflict of interest between them. Usually there will not be a conflict, but see Chapter 18 for an example of how this might arise.

There is not usually a conflict in acting for the seller and the seller's mortgagee as they both have the same objective in mind, i.e. successful redemption of the mortgage. Nor is there usually a conflict of interest in acting for the purchaser, and the purchaser's mortgagee, if the mortgagee is not a private person. However, there are two points that might arise:

(i) any defect in title that might affect the value of the property or the security of the mortgage must be made known to the mortgagee even though this might result in the mortgage offer being withdrawn;

(ii) any renegotiation in the terms of sale must be made known to the mortgagee, particularly any reduction in the purchase price. If the purchase price is reduced, a lender who is lending a substantial part of the price may also wish to reduce the amount of the loan. (For further details see Annex 25F on page 426 of the Law Society's Guide to the Professional Conduct of Solicitors, 7th Edition.)

If the mortgagee is a private person rather than an institutional lender, you cannot act for him and for the purchaser. This is because of the need to negotiate the terms of the mortgage.

3 Registered Title

Note: Unless it is otherwise indicated, a reference in this Chapter to 'the Act' is a reference to the Land Registration Act 1925.

3.1 Introduction

Conveyancing is bedevilled by the fact that the title to a legal estate may be either unregistered, or registered under the Land Registration Act 1925.

Whether or not the title is registered has no great effect on conveyancing procedure. The stages in the transaction remain the same. It does greatly affect investigation of title. It is also true to say that on some matters, such as the question of third-party interests in land, there is a different land law for registered title than there is for unregistered title.

If a title is unregistered, ownership of the legal estate is proved by the production of past conveyances, which show a transfer of the legal estate from one owner to another, and ultimately to the seller. The conveyances cannot guarantee ownership. To take a simple – although unlikely – example, a deed may be forged. A deed may also be voidable, for example, because it is a purchase of trust property by a trustee. However, the production of deeds, coupled with the fact that the seller is in possession of the house, i.e. either living there or receiving rent, usually offer assurance of ownership.

Just as the conveyances cannot guarantee ownership, neither can they guarantee that there are no third-party rights other than those mentioned in them. Some third-party rights may have been created by deeds predating those which the purchaser sees. Other third-party rights may have arisen independently of conveyances of the legal estate. A contract for sale, an option, an equitable interest arising from a resulting trust, would all be examples, as would an easement or restrictive covenant granted not in a conveyance of the land, but in a separate deed.

The Land Charges Act 1972, by providing for registration of some third-party interests affecting an unregistered title, does assist a purchaser who wishes to check on the existence of third-party rights. However, not all interests need to be registered under that Act. Nor can all interests that are registered necessarily be discovered by a purchaser. (Chapter 4 elaborates both these points.)

The purpose of the Land Registration Act 1925 is to simplify the investigation of title to a legal estate. If the title to, say, the freehold estate in Blackacre is registered, there is what amounts to a guarantee that the person named in the register as proprietor of the estate really does own it. This guarantee comes from what is known as the 'statutory vesting' (see

later). As regards third-party interests, a transferee for value of the registered title will take the estate subject only to interests that are protected by
an entry on the register, or that are 'overriding' interests. The reading of
the title deeds in unregistered conveyancing is, therefore, replaced by the
reading of the register.

Unfortunately, from the point of view of a purchaser, even in registered
conveyancing, reading the register is not enough. A transferee will take the
title subject to overriding interests, and an overriding interest is, by definition, an interest that is not entered on the register, but which will bind
anyone who acquires the title (s.3 of the Act). You will see that it is
the existence of overriding interests that introduces risk into registered
conveyancing.

3.2   How does a Title Come to be Registered?

Since 1925, bit by bit, counties or parts of counties have been designated as
areas of compulsory registration of title by Order in Council. (To tie this
down to a concrete example, Rochester upon Medway, in Kent, became
an area of compulsory registration on 1 March 1957). Indeed, as from 1
December 1990, the whole of England and Wales finally became an area of
compulsory registration.

The mere fact that an area is one of compulsory registration does not
mean that all the titles have to be registered. Only certain transactions
necessitate an application for first registration of the title to the legal estate.
Before 1 April 1998 these transactions were:

(i)   a conveyance on sale of the freehold estate;
(ii) an assignment on sale of a leasehold estate, provided the lease had
      over 21 years to run at the date of assignment;
(iii) the grant of a lease having over 21 years to run at the date of the grant
      (s.123 of the Act as amended by s.2(1) of the Land Registration Act
      1986).

'Sale' had its ordinary sense of selling for money. The 1925 Act expressly
said that if a piece of land was exchanged for other land, and equality money
was paid to even out the bargain, the land had been 'sold' (section 123(3)
before amendment by the Land Registration Act 1997). This left it
uncertain whether or not an exchange without equality money counted as
a sale.

However, if the following transactions take place on or after 1 April 1998,
they will now trigger first registration:

(i)   a conveyance of the freehold estate, whether by way of sale or gift; (As
      gifts will trigger first registration, exchange of a piece of land with an
      unregistered title for another piece of land will trigger first registra-
      tion, even although no equality money is paid.)

(ii) an assignment of a lease that at the date of assignment has more than 21 years to run, whether the assignment is by way of sale or a gift;

(iii) a grant of a lease for a term that is over 21 years at the date of the grant;

(iv) an assent of a freehold or of a leasehold that at the date of the assent has over 21 years to run;

(v) a legal first mortgage of a freehold estate or of a lease that at the date of the mortgage has over 21 years to run, provided the title deeds are deposited with the lender. (This triggers first registration of the freehold or leasehold estate, not just of the mortgage.)

The sale, gift, assignment, grant of lease or mortgage will have to be followed by application for first registration within two months of the disposition. In the case of a mortgage not linked to a purchase, it is the borrower who will have to pay for registration of his title to the mortgaged property.

At the end of the two months, if no application has been made, the disposition will become void. If the disposition was a transfer of ownership of a legal estate, the legal estate will revert to the transferor, who will hold it on a bare trust for the transferee. If the disposition was the grant of a lease or creation of a mortgage, the disposition will take effect as contract for value to grant the lease or mortgage.

The Registrar can extend the two month period if there is a good reason for the delay in applying for registration. If he does grant late registration, this will restore the legal estate and remove the need for a confirmatory conveyance or grant to replace the one that has become void.

These changes result from the amendment of s.123 by the Land Registration Act 1997.

It is essential, when buying an unregistered title, to check whether or not it is correct that the title is still unregistered. To do this you will need to know the date the area became one of compulsory registration, and to look at the nature of the transactions since that date, and when they took place. (You can obtain from the Land Registry a list of when areas became compulsory areas.)

Some examples may make these rules clearer.

Example 1

Samuel owns Blackacre, a house in Rochester. The title to it is unregistered. This is correct, because there has been no disposition of the house since he bought it in 1956, when Rochester was not an area of compulsory registration. Patience, the purchaser, is now buying the freehold. Samuel will prove his ownership of the legal estate by producing the 1956 conveyance of it into his name. The legal estate will vest in Patience at completion of the sale. Patience, having stamped the conveyance to her (see Chapter 2), must now remember the effect of s.123. She must apply for first registration of the freehold title. She will apply to the District Land Registry that deals with Kent, i.e. the one at Tunbridge Wells.

The Act does not compel her to apply for registration, but there is a sanction if she does not bother. The legal estate will revert to Samuel. He will hold it on trust for her, so she will retain the equitable interest and have every right to live in the house. She will feel the pinch, however, when she decides to sell. Her title will be defective, as she will not own the legal estate. She can acquire the legal estate by asking Samuel to re-convey it to her, and then applying for first registration within two months. A better alternative would be for her to apply to the Registry for late registration. The Registrar is likely to accept her application, and the effect of registration will be to re-vest the legal estate in her.

Example 2

Dorothea owns Wiseacre, a bungalow in Rochester. She bought it in 1956. In March 1998 she gives it to Ruth. Ruth is now selling it to Peter. The title to Wiseacre is unregistered. Peter must check:

- whether Dorothea's acquisition of Wiseacre should have been followed by first registration. We know that Rochester was not a compulsory area in 1956, so there was no necessity for Dorothea to apply for first registration when she bought her home.
- whether the gift to Ruth should have been followed by first registration. Although Rochester in 1998 was a compulsory area, a deed of gift made before 1 April 1998 did not trigger first registration. It is correct that the title is still unregistered.

Now imagine that the gift to Ruth is made in May 1998. A gift made on or after 1 April 1998 does trigger first registration. Ruth's failure to apply for first registration means that she no longer owns the legal estate, and her title is defective.

Example 3

Terry owns the lease of a house. His title to it is still unregistered. Terry dies in 1997. The lease passes to the executor of his will, Egbert. Egbert signs an assent which passes ownership to the beneficiary of the will, Ben. The passing of ownership to Egbert is not an event that triggers first registration, no matter what date this occurs. The assent will not trigger first registration if it is dated before 1 April 1998. It will if it is dated on or after 1 April and if Ben does not apply for first registration his title will become defective.

Example 4

Len owns a freehold farm and his title to it is unregistered. He grants a lease of it today to Giles. Within two months of the grant, Giles must apply for registration of his title to the leasehold estate. If he does not, he will lose the legal estate and only have the benefit of a contract for the grant of the lease. This will create an equitable lease, so Giles will not have to leave, but he will have to apply for late registration if he wishes to sell the lease.

Example 5

Betty owns a freehold house in York. The title to it is unregistered, as she bought it before York became a compulsory area. She now needs to raise money. She borrows from her bank, but has to mortgage the house. The mortgage must be followed by registration of Betty's title to the house, and registration of the mortgage in the charges register of Betty's title. The Act says that it is Betty who should apply for the registration. In fact it is the Bank who will probably take the responsibility of applying, but it will doubt-less be poor Betty who has to supply the registration fee.

3.3 Voluntary Registration

It is always possible for an estate owner to volunteer for registration of his title. Voluntary registration would clearly be convenient for an owner, such as a developer, who intends to sell his land off in parts. It will be easier to prove title to several purchasers, if the title is registered.

3.4 What Titles Can be Registered?

It is possible to register the title to

(a) the freehold estate
(b) a legal leasehold estate. It is not however, possible to register the title to a lease granted for twenty-one years or less.

These titles can be independently registered. It is also possible to regis-ter the title to an easement and to a mortgage or charge by deed. Such a registration will not be independent, but will be a registration against the title of the land affected. Registration of easements is discussed in Chapter 12. A mortgage or charge by deed can be registered as a registered charge in the charges register of the land affected.

3.5 The Effect of First Registration of a Title

The registration of a purchaser as proprietor of a legal estate automatically vests the legal estate in him (ss. 5 and 9 of the Act). This statutory vesting ensures that if you are dealing with the registered proprietor, you must be dealing with the owner of the estate.

Usually, the purchaser who has applied for first registration will already have acquired the legal estate on completion, so the statutory vesting merely confirms the pre-existing position. However, if, for example, the conveyance to the purchaser had been a forgery, no legal estate would have vested in him at completion, but will vest in him as soon as he is registered as proprietor. This example shows that registration can 'cure' a title.

3.6 Classes of Title

A proprietor can be registered with different classes of title. The class of title warns a purchaser about the extent of risk in dealing with that proprietor.

(a) Absolute Title to a Freehold Estate

Look at Example 1 in section 3.2. Patience has acquired the legal freehold estate on completion and must now apply for first registration of her title to it. She will do this by sending to the District Land Registry:

  (i) all the conveyancing documents, i.e. the pre-contract searches and enquiries (but not the local land charge search and additional enquiries), the contract, the requisitions on title, the land charge search certificates and the title deeds, together with a list in triplicate of all these documents;
 (ii) the Land Registry application form;
(iii) the fee.

The title will be investigated by the Registry staff. If there is nothing greatly wrong with the title, the Registrar will register Patience as proprietor of the freehold estate, with absolute title. (The date of registration is backdated to the date of application for first registration, Rule 42 of the Land Registration Rules 1925).

Section 5 of the Act says that a proprietor registered with an absolute title takes the legal estate, together with all rights appurtenant to it, subject only to:

  (i) *Incumbrances protected by an entry on the register* Suppose for instance, that on investigation of Patience's title, the Registrar realises that the title is subject to restrictive covenants, created by a past conveyance, and properly registered as a DII land charge. When he draws up the register of Patience's title, a notice of these covenants will be entered on the charges register. Patience now owns the legal estate subject to these covenants.

    Notice that when Patience's title was unregistered, she was bound by the covenants because they had been protected by registration as a land charge. Once her title is registered, she is bound by the covenants because they are entered on the charges register of the registered title. The registration as a land charge is now completely irrelevant. This is why it is so important for incumbrances existing at the date of first registration to be entered on the register (that is, unless they can take effect as overriding interests, e.g. legal easements). If the restrictive covenants were not entered on the charges register they would cease to bind Patience, as they would not be protected by an entry on the register, nor would they be overriding interests. The person with the benefit of the covenants would have been seriously prejudiced by the registration of the title. His remedy would be to apply for rectification of the title, to ensure that the covenants are entered in the charges register. (but see *Freer* v. *Unwins Ltd* [1976]).

Adverse interests entered on the register carry no risk to a purchaser of the registered title from Patience, as the interests are discovered by reading the register.

(ii) *Overriding interests*   This is the area of risk. An overriding interest is one that is not on the register, but which will bind a purchaser. These are discussed in 3.15. Some may be discovered by inspecting the land.

(iii) *Interests of beneficiaries, if the proprietor is not entitled to the land for his own benefit, but is holding it as a trustee*   These interests should not present a risk to a purchaser. If the proprietor holds as a trustee, this should be disclosed by a restriction on the proprietorship register. The purchaser can then arrange for the beneficiaries' interests to be overreached (if they exist behind a trust of land or a settlement under the Settled Land Act 1925) or otherwise satisfied. Even if there is no restriction on the register to warn the purchaser of the beneficiaries' interests, they may fail against him as being unprotected minor interests.

The danger is the presence of a beneficiary's interest which is not overreached, and which is an overriding interest because the beneficiary is occupying the land (see 3.16).

(b)   Absolute Title to a Leasehold Estate

By virtue of s.9 of the Act a person who is registered as proprietor of a lease with absolute title owns 'the legal leasehold estate, subject to the same rights as those affecting a freehold absolute title, but subject in addition to the covenants and obligations of the lease'.

The registration of an absolute leasehold title amounts to a guarantee not only that the proprietor owns the leasehold estate, but also that the lease was validly granted. Clearly, that guarantee can only be given if the Registrar knows that the landlord had the power to grant the lease. In other words, the Registrar needs evidence of the title to the freehold and to any superior leases. If the superior titles are registered, the evidence of title is in the registry and no further evidence need be deduced to the Registrar. For example, if L is registered as proprietor of the freehold estate with absolute title and grants a thirty-year lease to T, T will be registered as proprietor of the leasehold estate with absolute title.

(c)   Good Leasehold Title

If a person is registered as proprietor of a leasehold estate with good leasehold title, his position is the same as a proprietor of a lease with absolute title, but with an important exception. The registration does not guarantee that the lease is valid (s.10 of the Act). A purchaser knows that the proprietor owns the lease, and the purchaser can read the register and inspect the land to discover third-party rights, but the purchaser does not know if the lease is worth anything at all.

Why does an applicant for first registration only obtain a good leasehold title? Look at Example 4 in 3.2. Len cannot be forced by Giles to give details of his freehold title, unless there is a contract between them that the title will be deduced. When Giles applies for first registration he will be unable to give details of Len's title to the Registrar.

The Registrar, being unable to investigate the freehold title, cannot guarantee that the lease is valid. He can only give Giles good leasehold title. Look also at Example 3, where Ben has acquired the lease from the personal representative. Terry may have obtained no details of the landlord's title when he was granted the lease. No details can therefore be supplied by the personal representative to Ben. Ben will be registered with good leasehold title.

You can see that a good leasehold title is unattractive both to a purchaser and a purchaser's mortgagee. The problem is discussed in greater detail in Chapter 15.

(d)   Possessory Title to a Freehold or Leasehold Estate

A proprietor will be registered with a possessory title when the registrar is not satisfied with the documentary evidence of ownership. This may be because the applicant's title is based on his adverse possession (a squatter's title) or because he has lost his title deeds.

The drawback of a possessory title is that the registration is subject not only to everything to which an absolute title would be subject, but is also subject to any estate or interest that is adverse to the first proprietor's title and that exists at the date of first registration (ss.6 and 11 of the Act). In other words, the title is subject to the risk that X might pop up and claim that the registered proprietor has not been in adverse possession sufficiently long to extinguish X's estate or interest in the land. X's rights are overriding, so that a purchase from the registered proprietor may also be unable to deny X's superior claim to the land.

(e)   A Qualified Title

An applicant for registration with an absolute or good leasehold title may find that although the title is granted the Registrar wishes to put a qualification on it. This will be because the Registrar has found a particular flaw in it. For example, the Registrar may find that one of the conveyances was a purchase of trust property by one of the trustees. The beneficiaries of the trust could apply to the court to have this conveyance avoided. The Registrar would qualify the title, by stating that registration did not affect the rights of the beneficiaries.

A qualification can only be put on the title with the applicant's consent, but if the applicant refuses he may instead find himself registered with only possessory title. This is no more attractive to a purchaser than a qualified absolute title, as it is subject to *all* pre-registration claims. Qualified titles are rare.

3.7   Upgrading of Title

The rules for upgrading a title are contained in s. 77 of the Act, as amended by s.1 of the Land Registration Act 1986.

(a)   A good leasehold title can be upgraded to an absolute leasehold title if the Registrar has satisfactory evidence of the freehold and any superior leasehold title.

Look again at Example 4 in section 3.2. If Len sells the freehold title, the purchaser will have to apply for first registration. Details of the freehold title will then be available to the Registrar. He may register the purchaser from Len as proprietor of the freehold with absolute title, and change Giles' title to the lease from good leasehold to absolute. Giles could apply for the upgrading, or the Registrar could upgrade on his own initiative.

(b)   A possessory title can be upgraded to an absolute freehold title, or a good leasehold title, if either:

(i)   the Registrar is given satisfactory evidence of title; or
(ii)   if the title has been registered for at least twelve years and the Registrar is satisfied that the proprietor is in possession.

(c)   a qualified title can be changed to an absolute or good leasehold title if the Registrar is satisfied as to the title.

3.8   The Form of the Register

The register of the title is, confusingly enough, divided into three registers. (In Chapter 5 you will see a rather simplified version of a register of title.) Each registered title has its own title number.

The Property Register

This describes the property, e.g. 1 Smith Avenue. The description usually refers to the Land Registry filed plan. This plan only indicates the general boundaries of the land, but does not fix them exactly (rule 278 of the Land Registration Rules 1925). It describes the estate – i.e. freehold or leasehold. If the estate is leasehold, the register will include brief details of the lease (the date, parties, the term and its starting date).

The Proprietorship Register

This gives the name and address of the registered proprietor. It also gives the class of title, e.g. absolute, possessory, etc. You must realise that the class of title may change with a change of proprietor. O may be registered with an absolute title. If S enters into adverse possession against O, S may eventually be registered as the new proprietor, but possibly only with possessory title.

Any restriction will be entered on the proprietorship register. This is because a restriction reflects some sort of limitation on the proprietor's power to dispose of the land. Cautions are also entered here.

The Charges Register

Here are noted adverse interests such as restrictive covenants, easements and leases (unless the lease is an overriding interest). Also appearing here are registered charges (i.e. mortgages).

3.9   The Land Certificate

As has been seen in 3.6, when Patience applies for first registration of her title, she will send the title deeds to the Registry. When the registration of her as proprietor is completed, the deeds will be returned to her. These deeds no longer prove her title, and provided she has obtained an absolute title, there is no legal reason for preserving them, unless they reveal positive covenants (see Chapter 12). There will also be sent to her a land certificate. This is a copy of the register of title, sewn up in an imposing cover. This, in a sense, now plays the role of the title deeds – i.e. it is evidence of the registered proprietor's title. No transfer of the title, or other dealings, will be registered, unless the application for registration is accompanied by the land certificate. The land certificate is not quite the same as the title deeds, however. The register is the real evidence of title. Often the entries in the land certificate are exactly the same as the entries on the register as whenever the land certificate is deposited in the registry, the certificate will be brought up to date with the entries on the register. However, there are some entries which can be put on the register without the land certificate having to go into the Registry. These include cautions, and a notice protecting a spouse's rights of occupation under Family Law Act 1996.

3.10 The Charge Certificate

You may know that when an unregistered title is mortgaged for the first time, the lender nearly always takes control of the title deeds. It was felt necessary to reflect this practice in registered conveyancing. If a registered title is mortgaged by deed, the lender can register the mortgage as a registered charge. The application for registration is accompanied by the borrower's land certificate. The land certificate is then retained in the registry and a charge certificate is issued to the lender. The charge certificate will contain a copy of the entries in the register and a copy of the mortgage deed. If the title is mortgaged a second time, the proprietor of the second registered charge will have a second charge certificate.

3.11 Dealings with a Registered Title

The principle is this; that every registrable dealing with a registered title must itself be registered, or it will not pass a legal estate. What does this mean?

The following are registrable dealings:

(a) a transfer of the registered title. This may be on sale or by way of gift.
(b) a transmission of the title, e.g. to a personal representative on the death of the registered proprietor (see Chapter 10).
(c) a grant of a lease out of the registered title, if the lease is for over twenty-one years (see Chapter 16).
(d) the grant of a mortgage or charge by deed.
(e) the grant of an easement (see Chapter 12).

Here is a simple example. Susan owns the freehold estate in Blackacre. The title is registered. Susan sells Blackacre to Petunia. On completion, Susan will hand to Petunia the land certificate and a land registry transfer, executed by Susan. Petunia now owns the equitable interest in the land. She does not own the legal estate. Why not? Because no legal estate will pass until the transfer is registered. So the next step, once the transfer has been stamped with any *ad valorem* stamps necessary, and with the 'particulars delivered' stamp (see 2.16) is to apply for registration of the transfer. She will do this by sending the certificate, the transfer, application form and fee to the District Land Registry. Once Petunia is registered as the new proprietor the legal estate vests in her. There is no time limit for the registration of a dealing with the registered title, but Petunia should apply for registration before the priority period given by her pre-completion search expires (see 7.5).

3.12   Third-party Rights in Registered Title

A registered title can be subject to the same third-party rights (e.g. restrictive covenants, contracts, easements, mortgages, etc.) as unregistered title.

When the registered title is sold, will the purchaser be bound by these third-party interests? Does an owner of the third-party interest have to do anything to protect it?

Third-party interests in registered title fall into two categories, overriding interests and minor interests.

(a)   An Overriding Interest

This is defined by s.3 of the Act as an interest that is not entered on the register, but subject to which registered dispositions are by the Act to take effect. An overriding interest thus binds every purchaser of the title, yet cannot be discovered by reading the register. Most overriding interests are listed in s.70 of the Act and will be dealt with later.

(b)   Minor Interests

These are defined by s.2 and s.3 of the Act. The definition creates three categories:

  (i)   *Registrable dealings that have not been registered* So, looking at 3.11, we see that the equitable interest which Petunia acquires at completion is a minor interest until she registers the transfer.
 (ii)   *Equitable interests existing behind a trust of the legal estate* The interest of a beneficiary behind a settlement of the legal estate under Settled Land Act 1925 is a minor interest. The interest of a beneficiary behind a trust of land may be a minor interest.
(iii)   *Interests that are not created by registrable dispositions and which do not exist behind a trust.* Into this category will fall restrictive covenants, equitable leases, easements, contracts for sale, options, etc.

Notice that the categories of overriding and minor interest are not mutually exclusive. If a beneficiary behind a trust of land is living on the property, his interest will be overriding, by virtue of s.70(1)(g) of the Act. (However, the interest of a beneficiary behind a Settled Land Act settlement is always a minor interest, despite occupation. This is laid down by s.86(2) of the Act.)

Similarly, a lease granted for twenty-two years out of a registered title is a registrable disposition. Pending registration, the tenant will have a minor interest but if he goes into occupation, it will be an overriding interest, again because of s.70(1)(g).

3.13 The Need to Protect a Minor Interest

A minor interest, unlike an overriding interest, is at risk. It should be protected by some form of entry on the register. The reason for this can best be given by quoting part of s.20 of the Act.

> In the case of a freehold estate . . . a disposition of the registered land or a legal estate therein, including a lease thereof, for valuable consideration, shall, when registered, confer on the transferee or grantee an estate . . . subject to the incumbrances and other entries, if any, appearing on the register; and . . . to the overriding interests, if any, affecting the estate transferred . . . but free from all other estates and interests whatsoever.

S.23 is a similar provision dealing with the transfer of a registered leasehold title.

In other words, a transferee for value whether taking an outright transfer, or a mortgage, or a lease, will, when the disposition is registered, take free from any minor interest that is not protected by an entry on the register.

The transferee takes free of the minor interest, even though he knows of its existence. S.59(6) of the Act provides that a purchaser acquiring title under a registered disposition is not to be concerned with any matter or claim (not being an overriding interest) which is not protected on the register, whether he has or has not notice thereof, express, implied or constructive (but see *Lyus* v. *Prowsa Developments Ltd* [1982]*, the facts of which are given in the case notes to this chapter, for circumstances in which a purchaser did take subject to an unprotected minor interest because a constructive trust was imposed on him).

Note: When in a chapter an asterisk appears besides the name of a case, it signifies that the case is mentioned in the case notes to that chapter.

3.14 Methods of Protecting Minor Interests

(a) Registration

A registrable dealing should be registered. Until this is done, no legal estate is created or transferred.

(b) Notices

A notice is an entry of the interest on the charges register of the title affected. The land certificate must be deposited at the Registry before any notice is put on the register. This is why, generally speaking, the consent of the registered proprietor is needed before a notice can be used. However, we have seen that if the title is subject to a registered charge, the land certificate is retained in the registry. This makes it possible for a notice to be put on the register without the consent of the registered proprietor. The proprietor is told of an application to enter a notice, so he has an opportunity to object. (As an exception to this rule, a proprietor is not, for obvious reasons, told of a spouse's application for a notice to protect his/her rights of occupation under the Family Law Act 1996.)

A notice ensures that *if the interest is valid*, any transferee will take subject to that interest. The registered proprietor is, of course, always able to challenge the validity of the interest, as a notice cannot change a void or unenforceable interest into a valid one.

(c)   Cautions

If a notice cannot be used, because the land certificate is not deposited at the Registry, a caution must be used. When a cautioner applies for a caution to be entered, the application has to be accompanied by a statutory declaration, briefly describing the interest or right claimed by him. Unlike a notice, the caution itself does not set out the interest. A person reading the register will see merely 'Caution dated 1 April 1992 registered on 6 April 1992 in favour of Avril Printemps'.

The effect of lodging a caution is that the Registrar must inform the cautioner before he registers a dealing with the land. This gives the cautioner an opportunity to assert his claim in a hearing by the Registrar with usually one of three results:

(i)   the Registrar registers the dealing, but subject to the interest or rights of the cautioner;

(ii) the Registrar refuses to register the dealing at all;

(iii) the Registrar registers the dealing free of the cautioner's claim.

Theoretically, a caution is not as effective a protection as a notice. A notice ensures that the purchaser will, without more ado, take subject to the protected interest. A caution merely gives the cautioner a right to defend himself against a transferee by disputing the registration. A caution is intended to be used as a temporary form of protection only, for example to defend the cautioner's rights pending litigation between himself and the proprietor. Practically speaking, a caution on the register can paralyse dealings with the title, as no sensible purchaser will pay over the purchase price until the caution is removed from the register. The proprietor is thus forced either to come to terms with the cautioner or to litigate.

Warning off a caution A registered proprietor can apply to the Registrar to 'warn off' a caution. Notice is served on the cautioner, and if he does not object within the time-limit specified in the notice, the caution is cancelled. If the cautioner does object, the dispute will be settled by the Registrar or the court.

(d) Restrictions

A restriction is an entry on the proprietorship register that reflects the fact that the proprietor's powers of disposing of the land are limited in some way. It ensures that the proprietor complies with certain conditions before any transfer by him is registered. It therefore serves as a warning to a purchaser that these conditions must be satisfied before he buys.

Take, for example, what is called a 'bare trust'. Such a trust would exist if Ben, an adult, provided money for the purchase of land but for some reason did not want to hold the land in his own name. Legal ownership could be transferred to a nominee, who would be registered as the proprietor. This nominee, who we will call Nick, will hold the legal estate on a bare trust for Ben. The trust will be bare, because it will not carry the responsibilities that a trustee has when he holds on trust for several beneficiaries or for an infant. The bare trust will be a trust of land as defined by s.1 of the Trusts of Land and Appointment of Trustees Act 1996.

The trustee, Nick, will have the powers given to trustees of land by that Act including the power to sell. If Nick appoints another trustee to act with him, a sale by the two trustees could overreach Ben's interest, so that the purchaser takes free of any claim by Ben, whose rights would be switched to the purchase price.

In such a situation, both Ben and a potential purchaser need protection. Ben needs protecting from the possibility that the sale could take place without his consent. A purchaser needs protecting from the possibility that Nick will sell to him, concealing the trust and not appointing a second trustee. The purchaser could not defend himself against Ben's claim to be the equitable owner by saying that his interest had been overreached. The sale would not be by at least two trustees. Everything would depend on whether or not Ben was in actual occupation of the property at the time the sale was completed. If he were not, the purchaser would be safe, by virtue of ss.20 or 23 of the Act (see 3.13). If Ben were there, Ben would be safe by virtue of s.70(1)(g) of the Act (see 3.16).

At Ben's instigation, Nick could apply for a restriction to go on the register of title underneath Nick's name. The restriction would say, in effect, that no disposition by Nick will be registered unless the consent of Ben is obtained. This restriction would protect both Ben and a purchaser.

You can see from this example that a restriction may exist as much for the protection of a purchaser as for the owner of the third-party interest, as the restriction ensures that the necessary conditions are fulfilled to clear the third-party interest from the title. To labour the point, you must realise that the absence of the restriction does not prejudice a purchaser if the interest that should have been protected by it is a minor interest. However, failure to enter the restriction will prejudice the purchaser if the interest that should have been protected by it is an overriding interest. The purchaser has been deprived of the warning that there were conditions to be satisfied that *if* satisfied, would have cleared the interest from the title.

A restriction would have saved the bank (i.e. the purchaser) in *Williams and Glyn's Bank* v. *Boland* [1981]*, but would have saved the parents (i.e. the beneficiaries) in *City of London Building Society* v. *Flegg* [1988]* (see case notes at the end of this chapter).

A proprietor whose powers of disposition are limited does have a duty to apply for the appropriate restriction to be registered. The restriction can also be applied for by a person interested in the land. In some circumstances, the registrar is under a duty to put a restriction on the register, e.g. in the case of co-ownership. Examples of restrictions are given in Chapter 11.

(e)   Inhibitions

An inhibition prevents any dealing with the land at all. The only common one is the bankruptcy inhibition, which is put in the register when the receiving order is made.

3.15   Overriding Interests

Most overriding interests are set out in s.70 of the Act. Only the most common are dealt with here.

(a)   Easements

To quote s.70(1)(a) of the Act in full:

> Rights of common, drainage rights, customary rights (until extinguished), public rights, profits *a prendre*, rights of sheepwalk, rights of way, watercourses, rights of water and other easements not being equitable easements required to be protected by notice on the register.

The paragraph has been quoted in full, because the wording of it has led to controversy.

It is clear that a legal easement is overriding. Is an equitable easement? S.70(1)(a) excludes equitable easements 'required to be protected' on the register. It is not clear what this means. There is no *requirement* in the Act that equitable easements be protected by an entry on the register, although such protection is possible, using a notice or caution. It may be that 'required' means 'needing', i.e. an equitable easement that needs protection cannot be overriding. In *Celsteel* v. *Alton House Holdings Ltd* [1985] it was held that an equitable easement, openly exercised, is an overriding interest by reason of rule 258 of the Land Registration Rules Act 1925. Therefore, the only equitable easement that needs protection by an entry on the register is one not openly exercised, because such an easement is not an overriding interest. The need to register easements granted out of registered land is discussed in Chapter 12.

(b) Rights Acquired, or being Acquired under the Limitation Act 1980 (s.70(1)(f) of the Act)

If a title is unregistered, the effect of a squatter being in adverse possession of land for the limitation period is to extinguish the original owner's title, both as to the equitable interest and to the legal estate. If the title is registered, the adverse possession extinguishes the claim of the registered proprietor to the equitable interest. However, because of the principle that only registered dealings can transfer a legal estate, the registered proprietor will retain the legal estate until the register is rectified by entering the squatter as registered proprietor. Until rectification, the original proprietor will hold the legal estate on trust for the squatter.

If the original proprietor sells the title before rectification, the purchaser will take subject to the rights of the squatter. In other words, the transferee will be in no better position than the transferor.

(c) The Rights of a Person in Actual Occupation of the Land (s.7(1)(g) of the Act)

This is dealt with in 3.16.

(d) Local Land Charges (s.70(i)(i) of the Act)

As local land charges are overriding interests, it is as important for a purchaser of registered title to make a local land charge search, as it is for a purchaser of unregistered title. Details of the search are given in chapter 6.

(e) Leases Granted for a Term Not Exceeding Twenty-one Years (s.70(1)(k)

The title to a lease granted for twenty-one years or under is not registrable. The lease however, will be overriding, so that if the landlord's title is registered, any transfer of it will take effect subject to the lease.

In the case of *City Permanent Building Society* v. *Miller* [1952] the word 'granted' was seized on, and held to mean the creation of a legal estate. An informally created lease, taking effect only in equity, cannot, therefore, be overriding under s.70(1)(k). It could be overriding under s.70(1)(g).

It seems that as s.70(1)(k) makes the lease overriding, it will also make overriding any provision in the lease that affects the parties in their relationship of landlord and tenant. This would include an option to renew the lease, but would exclude an option to buy the landlord's reversion, as this is looked upon as a personal covenant (*Woodall* v. *Clifton* [1905]). However, such an option could be overriding under s.70(1)(g) (*Webb* v. *Pollmount* [1966]).

3.16   Section 70(1)(g) of the Act – Dangerous Occupiers

By virtue of s.70(1)(g), overriding interests include 'the rights of every person in actual occupation of the land, or in receipt of the rents and profits thereof save where enquiry is made of such person and the rights are not disclosed'.

At the start, it must be stressed that s.70(1)(g) does *not* say that occupation *creates* any rights. It is saying that *if* the occupier owns an interest in land arising under ordinary principles of property law, then occupation by the owner of the interest protects the interest and makes it overriding.

Uncle George who has been invited to live with the registered proprietor as a matter of family feeling is not a dangerous occupier, at least not to a purchaser. Uncle has no interest to assert against the purchaser, so his occupation is irrelevant.

However, an Uncle George who has contributed to the original purchase price, or who has paid for substantial improvements to the property and as a result of the work or contribution *owns part of the equitable interest*, is a dangerous occupier. He has an interest to assert, and his occupation makes the interest an overriding one. A purchaser who takes subject to the interest will be faced with the choice of living in the house with uncle, or re-selling the property and sharing the proceeds with him.

S.70(1)(g) makes not only an interest belonging to an occupier overriding, but also an interest belonging to anybody receiving rent from the land. So, for example, if the registered proprietor grants a lease to T, and T sublets to ST who lives on the property, both the sublease and lease are overriding interests.

Section 70(1)(g) can only make an interest overriding if it is one that by its nature is capable of surviving through changes in ownership. Neither a bare licence nor a contractual licence can, for this reason, be overriding interests (see *Strand Securities Ltd* v. *Caswell* [1965]). A licence backed by an estoppel could be overriding.

Although s.70(1)(1)(g) can make an interest overriding it does not otherwise change its character. It is now clear, for example, that the interest of a beneficiary behind a trust of land remains overreachable, even though the beneficiary is in occupation. Once the interest has been overreached, it cannot be asserted against the purchaser and s.70(1)(g) is irrelevant (*City of London Building Society* v. *Flegg* [1988]).

All interests belonging to the occupier are overriding, not just the interest which entitled him to occupy in the first place. So if a tenant is in actual occupation, not only is his lease overriding, but also an option in the lease for the purchase of the landlord's reversion (*Webb* v. *Pollmount* [1966]).

3.17   The Meaning of 'Actual Occupation'

What does 'actual occupation' mean? In unregistered title, the occupation of land by someone who claims on equitable interest is relevant because it may give constructive notice of the equitable interest to the purchaser. If the purchaser, after diligent enquiry and after inspection of the land, fails to discover the occupation, he will take free of the occupier's interest because he does not have notice of it.

Section 70(1)(g) has no such concept of notice within it. In *Williams and Glyn's Bank Ltd* v. *Boland* [1981] it was said that a person is in actual occupation of the land if 'physically present' there. Lord Scarman in his judgement stressed that the statute had substituted a plain factual situation for the uncertainties of notice. Lord Wilberforce stated that in registered land, if there was actual occupation and the occupier had rights, the purchaser took subject to them, and that no further element was material.

The result of the decision clearly is that a purchaser should make enquiry of any occupier that he discovers on the land, to ascertain if that occupier has an interest in it. The enquiry should be made of the *occupier* not the seller. It is only where enquiry is made of the occupier and the rights are not disclosed, that they cease to be overriding.

Yet even if a purchaser makes the most diligent search for occupiers, this may not be enough. Even if an occupier is undiscoverable (for example, deliberately concealed by the seller), his interest may bind the purchaser, if the occupier can be said to be physically present. It is the fact of occupation that matters, not its discoverability.

The meaning of occupation has been discussed by the House of Lords in *Abbey National Building Society* v. *Cann and amor* [1990] (see the case notes to Chapter 11). Mrs Cann claimed that she was in actual occupation on the day that the purchase of the house by her son, financed by a mortgage loan from the Building Society, was completed. On that day she was abroad, but her husband and son began to move her belongings into the house as the seller moved out. Her belongings were on the property for 35 minutes before completion of the purchase.

It was said by Lord Oliver that what was necessary for occupation might vary according to the nature and purpose of the property, but that occupation always involved some degree of permanence and continuity, and not a fleeting presence. A purchaser who before completion was allowed to go in to plan decorations or measure for furniture could not be said to be in occupation.

Mrs Cann's claim that she had been in occupation therefore failed.

3.18 When Must the Occupier be in Occupation?

It has been held that if his interest is to be overriding under s.70(1)(g), the occupier must be in occupation at the time the title is transferred to the purchaser (see again *Abbey National Building Society* v. *Cann and amor*, the facts of which are given in Chapter 11). Once the purchaser has taken subject to the interest, it is not necessary that the owner of the interest remain in occupation. His interest will continue to bind the purchaser, even though the owner of the interest then leaves. However, his interest will not bind a later transferee from the purchaser unless the owner of the interest resumes occupation before the transfer takes place (*London and Cheshire Insurance Co. Ltd* v. *Laplagrene Property Co. Ltd* [1971]).

3.19   The Undisclosed Trust of Land

Much of the litigation involving s.70(1)(g) has been in the context of an undisclosed trust of land, and is further discussed in Chapter 11.

Case Notes

Williams and Glyn's Bank Ltd. v. *Boland*

[1981]AC 487, [1980] 2 All ER 408, [1980] 3 WLR 138, 124 Sol Jo 443, 40 PCR 451.

Mr Boland was the registered proprietor of the family house. His wife had contributed a substantial sum towards the purchase of the house and as a result owned part of the equitable interest. Mr Boland, therefore, held the legal estate on trust for himself and his wife as tenants in common. No entry had been put on the register to protect the wife's interest. Mr Boland later borrowed money from the bank, and mortgaged the house to it. The bank made no enquiries of Mrs Boland. Mr Boland failed to keep up his mortgage payments, so the bank started an action for possession, with a view to selling the house. Could the bank obtain possession against Mrs Boland, or was it bound by her interest?

The bank could only be bound if her interest was an overriding one, under s.70(1)(g) of the Act. Counsel for the Bank raised two arguments in favour of the view that her interest could not be overriding.

One of the arguments was that Mrs Boland was not in 'actual occupation'. This argument was based on the view that underlying s.70(1)(g) were the old rules about notice, so that the occupation must be such as to make a purchaser suspicious. A purchaser would not be suspicious when he found a wife occupying a husband's house, as the marriage would be a sufficient explanation. This argument was resoundingly rejected. The section was to be interpreted literally. A person is in actual occupation of the house if physically present there.

The second argument used by counsel was also rejected, and is an argument that would not now be available owing to the effect of s.3 Trusts of Land and Appointment of Trustees Act 1996. The argument was based on the fact that s.70(1)(g) defines overriding interest as an interest subsisting in registered *land*. The trust in the Boland case was a trust for sale. At the time of the case, the interest of a beneficiary behind a trust for sale of land was traditionally regarded as not being in the land, but in the proceeds of sale. This was due to what was known as the equitable doctrine of conversion, based on the maxim that 'equity looks upon that as done which ought to be done'. As a trust should be carried out, land subject to a trust for sale should be regarded as already having been sold, and the interests of beneficiaries as existing in the fictional proceeds of a mythical sale. The House of Lords nevertheless held that Mrs. Boland's interest was capable of being overriding, as it would be unreal to deny that her interest was in the land, seeing that the object of the trust was in fact to provide her and her husband with a home. The doctrine of conversion was abolished by s.3

of the 1996 Act, and has not been missed except by its very close friends. A beneficiary behind a trust for sale of land has now an interest in the land.

City of London Building Society v. *Flegg [1988] AC 54, [1987] 3 All ER 435, [1987] 2 WLR 1266*

Mr and Mrs Maxwell-Brown, and Mrs Maxwell-Brown's parents, Mr and Mrs Flegg, proposed to buy a house for the four of them to live in. The Fleggs contributed £18000 towards the purchase price. The title was registered. The legal estate was transferred into the names of the Maxwell-Browns only, who held on trust for sale for themselves and their parents. Later, without the authority of the Fleggs, the Maxwell-Browns mortgaged the legal estate. The payments were not kept up, and the Building Society sought possession of the property. The parents claimed that they had an equitable interest in the house, by reason of their contribution towards its purchase, and that their interest bound the Society as the parents were in actual occupation. It was held in the House of Lords that the parents' interest could not be asserted against the Society, as the mortgage had been created by two trustees for sale and that consequently the interests of the beneficiaries had been overreached. Once the interests of the Fleggs had been overreached, they had no interest left in the land to be overriding.

Note that s.17 of the Trustee Act 1925 provides that a mortgagee lending money to trustees is not concerned to see that the trustees are acting properly. The validity of the mortgage, therefore, was not affected by the fact that the Maxwell-Browns were acting in breach of trust when creating it. The Fleggs could, perhaps, have put a restriction on the register, to the effect that no mortgage by the registered proprietors was to be registered without the Fleggs's consent (see Chapter 11).

Lyus v. *Prowsa [1982] 1 WLR 1044*

Land was sold by S to P expressly subject to X's contract to buy. The title was registered, but X was not in occupation and had not protected his minor interest by any sort of entry on the register. P then sold the land to Q, again expressly subject to the contract.

Q claimed that he was not bound by the contract, as it was an unprotected minor interest. It was held, however, that X could enforce the contract against Q.

The reason given was that P had held the land on a constructive trust for X. The judgement stressed that this was because it had been stipulated between S and P that P should give effect to the contract. No trust would have arisen if the sale had been said to be subject to the contract merely for the protection of S. The Land Registration Act 1925 could not be used as an instrument of fraud, so P could not claim to be released from the trust on the grounds that the contract had not been entered on the register. Q was bound by the trust, because he had bought with notice of it.

The decision has been criticised as having ignored provisions of the Land Registration Act. Section 74 of the Act, for example, states that a person dealing with a registered estate shall not be affected by notice of a trust. So Q should not have been affected by his notice of the constructive trust imposed on P. The decision was approved by the House of Lords, however, in *Ashburn Anstalt* v. *Arnold* [1987].

The same reasoning would apply to a conveyance of unregistered land. X's failure to protect his contract by registering it as a C(iv) land charge would usually ensure that the contract did not bind P, even though the conveyance by S to P said the land was conveyed subject to it. P would, however, be bound if the circumstances justified the imposition of a constructive trust.

Workshop

Attempt this problem yourself, then read the specimen solution at the end of the book.

Problem 1

You act for two brothers, Bill and Ben Brown, who have bought a freehold house, 15 Flowerpot Lane, for £65 000. They bought with the aid of a mortgage loan from the Bleaklow Building Society, for which you also act. The house was conveyed to the two brothers as tenants in common. In the conveyance they covenanted with the seller that no further buildings of any kind would be erected on the land. The transaction was completed yesterday.

1. What steps should you now take to ensure that the brothers will have a good title to the house?
2. What document will finally issue from the District Land Registry?

4 Unregistered Title: Third-Party Rights

This chapter serves as a reminder of the principles which decide whether or not a purchaser of *unregistered* land takes subject to a third party interest.

4.1 Is the Third Party's Interest Legal or Equitable?

When deciding whether or not the interest will bind a purchaser, the first question to decide is whether the interest is a legal interest or an equitable one. The reason is that generally speaking a purchaser of an unregistered title will take subject to legal estates and interests, whether he knows of them or not.

Interests capable of being legal include:

(a) A lease. Remember, however, that a lease is *capable* of being legal. In order to be so, it must have been granted by deed. A lease created by signed writing which does not amount to a deed will be equitable only (see Chapter 14 for the rules which now determine whether or not a document is a deed). The exception to this is a lease for 3 years or less at best rent without a premium, and giving an immediate right to possession. This can be created as a legal estate without a deed (Sections 52–4 of the Law of Property Act 1925.) So a periodic lease e.g. a weekly tenancy, will be legal, even though granted informally.

(b) An easement which is either perpetual, or granted for a term of years. (An easement for life can only be equitable.) Again, if the easement is to be legal, it must have been granted by deed.

(c) A legal mortgage or legal charge. However, if the mortgage or a legal charge is not protected by a deposit of title deeds with the lender, it is registrable under the Land Charges Act 1972, and will not bind a purchaser merely because it is legal (see later).

4.2 Is It Overreachable?

Equitable interests do not automatically bind a purchaser. So if faced with an equitable interest, the next questions will be, is the interest overreachable, and was it overreached?

Interests of beneficiaries behind a trust of the legal estate, or behind a settlement under the Settled Land Act 1925 are overreachable. If, for example, the legal estate is vested in two or more trustees of land, and they all convey, the interests of the beneficiaries will be overreached, and it is irrelevant whether the purchaser knew of their existence or not (see Chapter 11). If the sale had been by a single trustee, the interests would not be overreached, and would bind a purchaser who had notice of them.

4.3   Does the Land Charges Act 1972 Apply?

Once you have decided that the equitable interest has not been over-reached, the next questions to ask are, was the equitable interest registrable under the Land Charges Act 1972, and if so, was it registered? The principle is that if an interest is registrable, then if it is registered, it will bind a subsequent purchaser. If it is not registered, it will not. Registration is all. Of course, it is not quite as simple as that, and the principle is elaborated in section 4.5.

4.4   Notice

If you are left with an equitable interest that has not been overreached, and is not registrable as a land charge, you come to the well-known rule that the equitable interest will bind anyone who acquires the land with the exception of a *bona fide* purchaser for value of the legal estate without notice of the equitable interest.

Many equitable incumbrances are registrable under the Land Charges Act 1972, and if an interest is registrable under that Act, the concept of notice is irrelevant (see *Midland Bank Trust Co. Ltd* v. *Green* [1981]). The rule about the *bona fide* purchaser covers only those interests that do not fall within the Act. These interests include:

- restrictive covenants created before 1926;
- the interest of a beneficiary behind a trust of land that has not been overreached;
- an interest created by proprietory estoppel.

If a purchaser wishes to escape such an interest, he must prove that he bought a legal estate for value (this would exclude a donee, someone acquiring property by a gift in a will, and a squatter) without *notice*.

(a)   Actual Notice

Notice can be actual, i.e. the purchaser actually knows of the third-party interest. A purchaser may have actual notice of pre-1926 restrictive covenants because they are mentioned in the title deeds, and he reads them. (If he escapes actual notice because of his careless failure to read the title deeds, he will be fixed with constructive notice.)

(b)   Constructive Notice

The purchaser will be treated as having constructive notice of anything he does not know about but would have discovered had he made such enquiries as he ought reasonably to have made. It follows from this that if despite all reasonable conveyancing enquiries the equitable interest remains undiscovered, the purchaser takes free from it.

A purchaser risks constructive notice if he fails to see all the title deeds which he is entitled to see; for example, if he accepts title traced from a document that is not a good root, or accepts title traced from a good root less than 15 years old. He risks constructive notice if he fails to inspect the land.

Occupation   If someone other than the seller is occupying the land, that occupation gives constructive notice of any equitable interest the occupier owns. The occupation is suspicious; it throws doubt on the seller's claim of ownership, and should be investigated. (Do remember that if the occupier's equitable interest is registrable under Land Charges Act 1972, occupation is irrelevant. The interest will only bind the purchaser if it is registered.)

Not only is it possible to have constructive notice of the interest, it is also possible to have constructive notice of the occupation. In other words, if the purchaser, through his failure to make proper inspection of the property, fails to discover the occupier, he has constructive notice of the occupation, and through it, constructive notice of any equitable interest the occupier owns (see *Midland Bank Ltd* v. *Farmpride Hatcheries Ltd* [1980] and *Kingsnorth Trust Ltd* v. *Tizard* [1986]).

If the seller is in occupation, but with another, the occupation by that other may also give constructive notice of any equitable interest he owns. It still depends, of course, on the occupier being discoverable by ordinary conveyancing enquiries. It was said in *Kingsnorth Trust Ltd* v. *Tizard* that a purchaser is not under a duty to pry into drawers and wardrobes in a search for signs of occupation. However, it was also said that a purchaser who inspected the property by a pre-arranged appointment with the seller had not made proper enquiries, as the seller had been given an opportunity to conceal signs of occupation. Apparently, according to the judgement, only by calling on the seller unawares, and thoroughly inspecting the property, can a purchaser escape constructive notice.

The case also suggests that if the purchaser has reason to believe that the seller is married, then an enquiry must be pursued as to the possibility that the spouse may have an equitable interest, whether the spouse is in occupation or not.

(c)   Imputed Notice

Any notice, actual or constructive, received by the purchaser's agent (e.g. solicitor, licenced conveyancer or surveyor) in the course of the transaction is imputed to the purchaser.

4.5 The Land Charges Act 1972 (Formerly 1925)

(a) Registrable Interests

The Act permits registration of certain interests affecting the title to
unregistered land. Not all the interests registrable under the Act are listed
here but only those most likely to be revealed by a search made by a
purchaser.

(i) *A petition in bankruptcy* This is registered in the register of pending
actions. A search certificate will reveal the entry PA(B).

(ii) *A receiving order in bankruptcy* This is registered in the register
of writs and orders, and a search certificate will reveal the entry
WO(B).

(iii) *A land charge class C(i)* This is a legal mortgage unprotected by a
deposit of title deeds with the lender. A mortgage protected by
deposit of title deeds cannot be registered as a land charge, the idea
being that the absence of the title deeds is itself enough to alert the
purchaser to a possible claim against the land.

(iv) *A land charge class C(iii)* This is defined as an equitable charge not
protected by deposit of title deeds. This class includes the purchaser's
lien for a deposit paid to the seller or seller's agent, and the seller's
lien for any unpaid purchase price provided that he parted with the
deeds on completion. It is uncertain whether an equitable mortgage
of the legal estate should be protected by being registered as a C(iii)
land charge, or as a C(iv) (being a contract for the grant of a legal
mortgage).

(v) *A land charge class C(iv)* This is defined by the Act as 'a contract
by an estate owner or by a person entitled at the date of the contract
to have a legal estate conveyed to him to convey or create a legal
estate, including a contract conferring expressly or by statutory implication a valid option to purchase, a right of pre-emption or any other
like right'.
This covers

(aa) A contract to sell the freehold. It also includes a subcontract.
Suppose Sarah contracts to sell Blackacre to Pauline, who
immediately contracts to resell it to Rosemary. Pauline can
register a C(iv) against Sarah. Rosemary can also register a
C(iv), as Pauline is a person entitled to have the legal estate conveyed to her. However, registration of the contract must be not
against Pauline's name, but against Sarah's, as the Act requires
a land charge to be registered against the name of the estate
owner. It is Sarah who owns the legal estate (see *Barrett* v. *Hilton
Developments Ltd* [1975]).

(bb) A contract to assign a lease.

(cc) A contract to grant a lease.

(dd) An option to buy the freehold or a lease, an option to renew a lease, and an option given to a tenant to acquire his landlord's reversion.

(ee) A right of pre-emption. A right of pre-emption is created, for example, when X contracts that if he wishes to sell the land, he will first of all offer it for sale to Y, before putting it on the open market. By contrast, an option is the right for Y to buy X's land, whether X wishes to sell or not. It was decided in *Pritchard* v. *Briggs* [1980] that a right of pre-emption, unlike an option, does not in itself create any interest in land capable of binding a purchaser. It is a personal right. However, when the circumstances occur which make the right of pre-emption exerciseable, (for instance, in the above example, when X puts the land up for sale) the right of pre-emption ripens into an option. A C(iv) land charge registered when the *right of pre-emption was created* will protect the option, and ensure that the option binds the purchaser.

(ff) A contract by a tenant to surrender his lease before seeking to assign it (*Greene* v. *Church Commissioners for England* [1974]).

(gg) An equitable lease.

(hh) A contract for the grant of a legal easement.

(vi) *Class D(ii) A restrictive covenant created after 1925* (but not one made between landlord and tenant).

(vii) *Class D(iii) An equitable easement* If the easement is equitable solely because it was not granted by deed, the correct head of registration appears to be C(iv), as the defective grant is treated as a contract for the grant of a legal easement. It is for the same reason that an equitable lease is registered as a C(iv) land charge. Class D(iii) seems to cover only an equitable easement that is incapable of being legal, e.g. an easement for life.

(viii) *Class F A spouse's rights of occupation under the Family Law Act 1996* Sections 31 to 33 give a spouse who does not own the legal estate in the matrimonial home rights of occupation in that home. These rights are capable of binding a purchaser, provided (in the case of an unregistered title) they are protected by the registration of a class F charge.

(b) System of Registration

The system of registration adopted in 1925 was not registration against the land affected, but against the name of the person who owned the legal estate at the time of registration. This is unfortunate as a registration can only be discovered by a search against the right name. For example, suppose that since 1925 the freehold in Blackacre has been conveyed by the following deeds:

1928 a conveyance by A to B
1954 a conveyance by B to C
1969 a conveyance by C to D
1973 a conveyance by D to E

A purchaser from E sees only the 1973 conveyance, as this is fifteen years old. He enquiries of the Chief Land Registrar if any land charges are registered against the names of D and E. The reply is 'no'. Suppose, though, that in 1928, in the conveyance from A, B gave a restrictive covenant to A, burdening the land that B had just acquired from him. A, being the person with the benefit of the covenant, would have hastened to register a D(ii) land charge against B's name. Only a search against B's name will reveal that registration. The purchaser cannot search against B's name because he does not know it, yet the convenant will bind the purchaser, as it is registered. So a purchaser takes subject to all land charges registered since 1925, but only has the opportunity to discover the recent ones.

This is the problem of what is called 'the pre-root land charge'. It is mitigated by:

 (i) The practice of every deed mentioning existing incumbrances in the habendum. It is likely that the 1973 conveyance would say that Blackacre was conveyed to E 'subject to the covenants created by a deed dated 29 February 1928 made between A of the one part and B of the other part'. The purchaser can add these two names to his search.
 (ii) The duty of the seller to disclose all incumbrances affecting the present title, even those created pre-root.
 (iii) The possibility of compensation under s.25 Law of Property Act 1969 (see Chapter 20).

(c)   Name?

Although the Act requires registration against the 'name' of the estate owner it does not say what is meant by 'name'. The case of *Diligent Finance Co. Ltd* v. *Alleyne* (1972) established the convenient rule that the name against which registration is to be effected is the name contained in the conveyancing documents.

A registration against an incorrect version of this name will not bind someone who searches against the correct name, and obtains a clear certificate of search. In the Alleyne case, a wife registered a class F charge against Erskine Alleyne. This registration did not bind a mortgagee, who searched against the husband's full name Erskine Owen Alleyne, the version of the name that appeared in the deeds. This shows how the rule in the Alleyne case can catch out a person who cannot see the deeds.

Although a registration against an incorrect version of the name will not bind someone who searches against the correct version, it has been said that it will bind someone who does not search at all, or someone who searches against *another* incorrect version. In *Oak Co-operative Building Society* v. *Blackburn* [1968] the name against which the land charge should have been registered was Francis David Blackburn. The charge was registered against the name of Frank David Blackburn. The purchaser applied for a search to be made against the name of Francis Davis Blackburn and obtained a clear search certificate. It was held that the purchaser could not rely on the search certificate, but took subject to the charge.

(d) Effect of Non-Registration

An unregistered land charge is void against a purchaser for value of any interest in the land. Exceptions to this are land charges C(iv), and D(i)(ii) and (iii), which are void against a purchaser for money or money's worth of a legal estate. The only difference in the two types of consideration is marriage, which provides value but not money's worth.

The difference between a purchaser of any interest, and the purchaser of a legal estate is of more significance. An unregistered class F land charge is void against both a legal and an equitable mortgagee. An unregistered estate contract is void for non-registration only against a legal mortgagee.

It seems that once a land charge is void against a later purchaser, it is also void against anyone who claims through the purchaser. For example, suppose that Morgan owns Blackacre, and gives Owen an option to buy it. Two weeks later, Morgan conveys Blackacre to Pritchard. Then Owen registers a C(iv) land charge. Pritchard sells Blackacre to Ross. Does Ross take subject to the option? It was registered before he bought it. However, he probably shares Pritchard's immunity. After all, it means little to Pritchard that he *owns* free of the option if he cannot also *sell* free of it.

(e) The Owner at the Date of Registration

The Land Charges Act says that a land charge is to be registered against the name of the estate owner whose estate is intended to be affected by the registration. This means the name of the person who owns the legal estate at the date of registration, not the estate owner who created the land charge.

For example, suppose that in 1995 Alec conveys Blackacre to Bella. Bella covenants in the conveyance to use the land only for residential purposes. The convenant is given to preserve the value of neighbouring land still belonging to Alec. Alec should register a D(ii) land charge against the name of Bella without delay. Suppose he does not? If Bella *sells* the land to Catherine, then as we have seen, there is probably no point in Alec registering the land charge now. The covenant is void against Catherine and probably against her successors too. However if Bella makes a *gift* of it to Catherine, there would be a point to Alec registering the charge, even at this late stage, as it has not yet become void for non-registration. But notice that if Alec does decide to register it, he must register it against the name of Catherine, not against the name of Bella.

(f) Registration against a Dead Estate Owner

Before the Law of Property (Miscellaneous Provisions) Act 1994 came into effect, there was a problem when an estate owner died. Suppose that, as in the above example, Bella gave the restrictive covenant and then died before Alec registered his land charge. Alec could not now register it against her name as she has ceased to be the estate owner. Alec would have to register it against the name of her personal representative, or if no grant of representation had yet been made and Bella had died intestate, against the President of the Family Division. This rule created a trap for Alec, who possibly had no idea that Bella was dead, or if he did, had no idea that he could not register against her name. It could also create a trap for a purchaser, who never dreamt of searching for a registration against the President. The rule has been changed by s.15 of the 1994 Act which amends s.3 of the Land Charges Act 1972 by adding the words 'Where a person has died and a land charge created before his death would apart from his death have been registered in his name, it shall be so registered notwithstanding his death.'

This amendment applies to an application for registration made on or after 1 June 1995.

Unfortunately the effect of the amendment is not absolutely clear. Suppose Bella dies in March 1998. It is clear that Alec can still register the land charge against her name. But suppose that in May 1998 her personal representative takes out a grant of representation. He is now the estate owner. Can Alec still register the land charge against Bella, or should he now register it against the name of the personal representative? The wording of the amendment seems to support registration against Bella's name. But for her death, registration would be against her name.

If this interpretation of the amendment is wrong and from May the registration must be against the name of the personal representative, it will create a problem for Alec, who must discover the date of the grant and the name of the personal representative, and has no easy way of doing this, short of using the standing search facility at the Probate registry.

The uncertainty also creates a problem for any later purchaser of the land. When he searches against the name of an estate owner whose ownership of the legal estate has passed on his death, he should ask for the search against that name to continue until ownership has been conveyed to a purchaser for money. For example, if Alec conveys to Bella in April 1995, and she dies in March 1998, and her personal representative takes out a grant in January 1999, and sells to Petroc in 2000, a later purchaser should ask for the search against Bella's name to cover the years 1995 to 2000 inclusive as a registration against her name in any of those years might be effective. The purchaser will also search against the name of the personal representative for the years 1999 to 2000 inclusive, both in case the registration of a land charge created by Bella can be effectively registered against the personal representative's name, and also in case the personal representative has himself created a land charge.

(g)   A Search at the Land Charges Registry

This is dealt with in Chapter 9.

Workshop

Questions needing a knowledge of the Land Charges Act will be asked at the end of later chapters.

5   Drafting the Agreement for Sale

5.1   Introduction

In order to draft the agreement for sale, the seller's solicitor must have a thorough knowledge of his client's title, information about the property (almost invariably culled from the client rather than by looking at the property) and must know anything that has been agreed between his client and the purchaser, for example the fact that the sale includes curtains (see 1.3).

5.2   Drafting an Agreement to Sell a Registered Title

(a)   Introduction

Suppose that you are the solicitor or licensed conveyancer instructed by Harry Mark to sell his house, 232 Main Road. It is clear from the estate agent's particulars and from what Harry tells you, that he owns a small end-of-terrace house, built about 1900, that fronts onto the road. Harry lives alone there. In response to your questions about the possibility of any neighbours having rights over the property, he tells you that his neighbours, who live at 234, have the right to cross his backyard in order to reach the side entrance which runs between numbers 232 and 230. This side entrance belongs to number 230, but Harry tells you that a right to use it was granted in 1980 to the then owners of 232 and 234, in return for the surrender by them of a right-of-way across the back garden of 230 to Ship Lane.

The house is mortgaged to Harry's bank, but the bank has told you that the title is registered and you have obtained office copy entries.

Harry wants to take various plants from the garden when he moves, particularly some shrub roses. The purchase price of the house is £72000 but he is also selling the curtains and the wardrobes. These are not fitted wardrobes, but are being left behind because they are too big to get down the stairs without being dismantled. The price agreed for the curtains and wardrobes is £1000.

Look at the office copy entries and filed plan shown opposite and on page 58.

OFFICE COPY ISSUED BY THE MUNBRIDGE WELLS LAND REGISTRY SHOWING THE SUBSISTING ENTRIES ON
THE REGISTER ON 1 JANUARY XXXX UNDER S.113 OF THE 1925 ACT THIS COPY IS ADMISSIBLE IN
EVIDENCE TO THE SAME EXTENT AS THE ORIGINAL.

TITLE NUMBER: K000000

HM Land Registry

Edition date: 19th March 1981

Entry No	A. PROPERTY REGISTER containing the description of the registered land and the estate comprised in the Title
	COUNTY **DISTRICT** KENT HOPE'S BOTTOM
1.	(17 October 1951) The Freehold land shown edged with red on the plan of the above Title filed at the Registry and being 232 Main Road, Kent (HO19 2EX)
2.	(30 April 1980) The Property has the benefit of a right-of-way granted by a deed dated 15 April 1980 made between (1) Express Developments Limited and (2) Betty Booper

Entry No	B. PROPRIETORSHIP REGISTER stating nature of the Title, name, address and description of the proprietor of the land and any entries affecting the right of disposing thereof **TITLE ABSOLUTE**
1.	(19 March 1981) Proprietor(s): HARRY MARK of 232 Main Road, Hopes Bottom, Kent (HO19 2EX)

Entry No	C. CHARGES REGISTER containing charges, incumbrances etc. adversely affecting the land and registered dealings therewith
1.	(17 October 1961) By an agreement dated 21 February 1961 made between Lilian Hopwood and the County Council of the Administrative County of Kent, a strip of land fronting Main Road comprising three square yards was dedicated as part of the public highway.
2.	(19 March 1981) Charge dated 28 February 1981 to secure the monies including the further advances therein mentioned.
3.	(19 March 1981) Proprietor - Midland Bank plc of 19 Pessimist Street, Hopes Bottom, Kent (HO9 4LX)

H.M. LAND REGISTRY	TITLE NUMBER		
	K 000000		
ORDNANCE SURVEY PLAN REFERENCE		SECTION Q	Scale
COUNTY KENT DISTRICT HOPES BOTTOM			© Crown copyright 1975

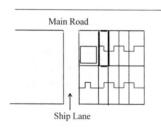

N.B. The thick black line represents red edging

The property register mentions the right of way over the side entrance of number 230. As this was granted to benefit registered land, the deed granting it was sent to the Land Registry, and the easement was registered in the property register of the benefited land. (If the title to number 230 was also registered, the easement should also appear in the charges register of that title (see Chapter 12)). As the grant is not set out in full in the property register, the purchaser will want to see a copy of this deed. We can obtain an office copy of it from the Registry.

There is no mention of the right of way belonging to number 234 over the backyard of our client's house. Remember the age of the property. The right was probably never expressly granted, but arose by prescription, i.e. by virtue of long use. It would have existed as a legal easement when the title to number 232 was first registered, but as there was no documentary evidence of it, no entry was put on the charges register. Nevertheless, it will still be enforceable against a purchaser from Harry, as it is an overriding interest (see 3.15).

Now you can start to draft the agreement.

(b) The Form of the Agreement

Look at the form of agreement in Appendix A to this book. This is the standard form of Agreement which must be used if you are following the protocol. You are likely to use it even if you are not. It incorporates what are known as the Standard Conditions of Sale (3rd Edition). See Appendix B.

The front page of the agreement, when completed, will give details of the property, the seller's title to it, and other terms of the bargain. The back page lists the conditions of sale. The conditions are the terms upon which the property is sold. There is a distinction to be drawn between the standard conditions and the special conditions. The standard conditions have been drawn up by the Law Society and the Solicitors' Law Stationery Society Ltd who own the copyright. They are designed to be suitable for both domestic and commercial conveyancing, and cover eventualities likely to be common to most transactions. The special conditions are those written into the contract by the person drafting it, to deal with matters peculiar to the particular transaction (although some special conditions are already printed onto the agreement form in a helpful manner).

Read the printed special condition 1. It expressly incorporates the standard conditions into the contract. The Law Society recommends that if the standard conditions are not actually printed on the form of agreement, then a copy of them should be attached to it. This will ensure that s.2 of the Law of Property (Miscellaneous Provisions) Act 1989 is satisfied (see 5.10).

(c) Date and Parties

Still looking at the form, you will see that the first blank to be filled in is the date. *Do not fill this in.* The agreement will be dated when the two parts are exchanged, probably with the date of exchange.

The next part to fill in shows the names of the parties. Your investigation of title and enquiries of Harry have satisfied you that he is the beneficial owner of the legal estate. There seems to be no equitable interest to overreach, and no need for the appointment of another trustee to act with him (see Chapter 11 for circumstances in which the appointment of a second trustee would be necessary). Harry or the estate agents will have told you the purchaser's name.

(d) The Property

You then have to draft the description of the property. This must be done carefully, for if the seller misdescribes the title (e.g. calls a sub-lease a head-lease) or the property (e.g. says it is 100 acres when it is only 75) he will inevitably break his contract. He will not be able to convey what he has contracted to convey. This particular breach of contract is called misdescription and is dealt with in Chapter 19.

The three things to bear in mind are:

(i) stating the estate;
(ii) describing the extent of the property;
(iii) stating any rights that benefit the property.

So, if number 232 had been an unregistered title, a satisfactory description would have been, 'The freehold property known as 232 Main Road, Hope's Bottom, Kent HO19 2EX, together with the benefit of a right-of-way over part of number 230 Main Road, so far as the same was granted by a deed dated 15 April 1980 made between (i) Express Developments Limited and (ii) Betty Booper'. Of course, a copy of the 1980 deed would have to accompany the draft contract, otherwise the purchaser's solicitor would find that part of the description meaningless. No plan would be used. The boundaries of number 232 are well-established and no map is needed to determine them. Most urban properties can be described by postal address alone.

In fact the title to number 232 is registered. This need not make any change to the particulars at all. However, in registered title, it is usual to see the particulars drafted in this way: 'the freehold property known as 232 Main Road, Hope's Bottom, Kent HO19 2EX, as the same is registered at HM Land Registry with absolute title under Title Number K000000'. This has the advantage of making it clear that the seller is only contracting to convey the land that is registered under the title. (If the registered title does not include all the land that the purchaser hoped to buy, the seller cannot be accused of misdescription.) An office copy of the entries on the register and of the filed plan will accompany the draft contract, and a copy of the 1980 deed. Nothing is said about the 1980 right-of-way in the particulars, as the contract is promising the land described in the property register, and the property register mentions the easement. (Notice that it is in fact never essential to mention easements that benefit the land. They will pass to the purchaser on completion anyway, as being part of the land conveyed. If there is any doubt about the enforceability of the easement against the neighbouring land, the easement should not be mentioned at all, or else the doubt should be made clear in the contract.)

(e)   Root of Title/Title Number

A contract only specifies a root of title if the seller's title is unregistered. Your client's title is registered, so you merely state the title number. Had Harry's title been other than absolute, you should have stated the class of title. The reason is that it has been held that if a title is described in the agreement merely as registered, the purchaser is entitled to assume that it is registered with absolute title. If the seller is registered only with possessory or good leasehold title, it is true that that will be disclosed by the accompanying copy entries, but a special condition puts the question of disclosure beyond doubt (Re Brine and Davies' Contract c1935).

If you have already stated the title number and class of title in your description of the property (see b), nothing need be written here at all.

(f) Incumbrances

Look at standard condition 3.1.1 (see Appendix B). The seller is selling the property free from incumbrances other than those that are listed in condition 3.1.2. This says that the property is being sold subject to incumbrances that are mentioned in the agreement, and also those that are discoverable by inspection of the property before the contract. Harry might argue that this right-of-way is discoverable by inspection, perhaps because of a gate in the wall dividing number 234 from number 232, but the purchaser may later dispute this. The safest thing to do is to mention the easement in the agreement. You will do this by giving details of it under the heading 'Incumbrances' on the front page of the agreement. You might say something like 'a right belonging to the owners and occupiers of number 234 to walk across the backyard of the Property to and from the side entrance running along the boundary of the Property and number 230, Main Road'. You could also add that there is no documentary evidence of the right-of-way, but that it has been exercised for many years, and is believed to have arisen through prescription. Now read special condition 2. The sale is now subject to this right-of-way.

The subject of disclosure of incumbrances is dealt with in greater detail later in this chapter.

(g) Title Guarantee (full/limited)

A person who disposes of a freehold or existing leasehold estate or who grants a lease can, if he wishes, give a title guarantee to the person acquiring the property. The guarantee will be given in the conveyance or transfer which passes ownership to the purchaser. This will be done by saying in the transfer that the seller transfers 'with full title guarantee' or 'with limited title guarantee'. These phrases then import into the transfer covenants for title set out in the Law of Property (Miscellaneous Provisions) Act 1994.

The preceding agreement for sale may promise that such a guarantee will be given in the transfer. This is an example of the many occasions when the contract will govern and control the wording of the later transfer or conveyance (see Chapter 12 for further examples).

Standard Condition 4.5.2 promises that the seller will transfer with full title guarantee, i.e. that the words 'with full title guarantee' will appear in the transfer. This is often repeated on the front page of the agreement by deleting 'limited' from the printed special condition or by saying 'the seller will transfer with full title guarantee.' If the seller only wishes to give a limited title guarantee in the transfer, he should delete 'full' and say 'the seller will transfer with limited title guarantee only'. This will then override the standard condition. A seller may be unwilling to give any title guarantee at all, and should then delete both 'full' and 'limited' and say 'the seller will not transfer with any title guarantee, and standard condition 4.5.2 does not apply to this contract' or words to that effect.

As Harry's title is registered, and he has lived on, and knows, the property, there is no reason why he should not be willing to give a full title guarantee, and that is certainly what the purchaser will expect.

(Note: a fuller explanation as to what covenants are implied when a title guarantee is given is in Chapter 20.)

(h) Completion Date

The completion date will be inserted when agreements are exchanged, and is obviously a matter of negotiation between the seller and purchaser. If this clause is not completed, standard condition 6.1.1 provides that the date for completion will be 20 working days after the date of the contract.

Whether the completion date is fixed by a special or by the standard condition, standard condition 6.1.2 states that if the money due on completion is received after 2.00 p.m. on that day, completion is for the purposes of standard conditions 6.3 and 7.3 to be treated as taking place on the next working day. Working days are defined by standard condition 1.1.1 to exclude weekends and bank holidays. So, for example, suppose completion date is Friday, 31 March. The purchase price is not received from the purchaser until 3.30 p.m. on Friday. For most purposes – e.g. the dating of the conveyance or transfer – completion took place on Friday. However, under condition 6.3 the outgoings will be apportioned as if completion took place on Monday, 3 April and the purchaser will under condition 7.3 have to pay interest for late completion.

(i) Contract Rate

This clause is used to agree a rate of interest for the contract. This rate of interest is relevant to calculate the interest payable on late completion (see standard condition 7.3). The rate of interest can be specified by a special condition. It must not be too high, or it may deter a prospective purchaser from entering into the contract. Remember too that if Harry is responsible for the delay in completion, he will be paying the same rate. The point is to have the contract rate something higher than the rate charged by banks for a bridging loan. This encourages a purchaser to complete promptly, as it will be cheaper for him to obtain a bridging loan than to delay completion. If a special condition is felt necessary, it will probably specify a figure that is something above the base rate from time to time of a chosen bank, e.g. '4 per cent per annum above the base rate from time to time of the Midland Bank plc'.

If a rate is not set by a special condition, standard condition 1.1.1 says that the rate is 'the Law Society's interest rate from time to time in force'. The Law Society sets a rate for this purpose which is published in every issue of the *Law Society's Gazette*. It is a figure 4 per cent above the base rate of the Law Society's own bank, which is Barclays. The rate set by the standard condition will, therefore, generally be acceptable, and only peculiar circumstances will make it necessary to set the rate by a special condition.

If conveyancers are prepared to accept the standard condition, it will have the advantage of ensuring that every contract in a chain of transactions will have the same interest rate applying to it. However, this is not always desirable if there is a big disparity in the purchase prices (see Chapter 18).

(j) The Purchase Price, Deposit and Amount Payable for Chattels

The purchase price is the amount payable for the land, so in Harry's case it is £72000. Land includes fixtures. Standard condition 2.2.1 provides for the payment by the purchaser of a deposit of 10 per cent of the purchase price. Unless this is altered by a special condition (it is now quite common for the purchaser to pay less than 10 per cent) the figure here will obviously be £7200.

There is then added the price payable for the chattels (£1000) so the balance payable on completion is £65800.

It is important for the purchaser that the total of £73000 to be paid is correctly apportioned between the land and the chattels. One reason is that stamp duty is only paid by the purchaser on the consideration paid for the land. Another reason is that the deposit is 10 per cent of the purchase price paid for the land, not for the chattels.

(k) The Agreement

The front page concludes with the promise of the seller to sell, and the purchaser to buy.

(l) Printed Special Conditions

Now turn to the back page of the form. There is no reason in this transaction to change the first three of the four special conditions already printed here.

(m) Special Condition – Fixtures and Chattels

You know that it has been settled between Harry and the purchaser that Harry can remove the roses, but is selling the carpets and wardrobes.

The underlying law is that once Harry has contracted to sell the land, he cannot remove any part of it, unless the contract permits him to do so. Plants are generally part of the land, so the contract must give Harry the right to remove the roses. A dispute can arise as to whether a particular item is a chattel (and not therefore part of the land, so removable before completion unless the contract says otherwise) or a fixture (and therefore part of the land, so not removable). The legal definition of a fixture is that it is a chattel which is fixed to the land and has lost its identity as a chattel and become part of the land. The definition is easy to state, but not to apply. The initial test is that of fixing. If the chattel is fixed to the land or to the house on the land, it is presumed to be a fixture. If not fixed, it is presumed to be a chattel. This test can however, be upset by a finding of intention. An item may not be fixed, yet rank as a fixture because it was intended to become part of the land. A dry stone wall would be a fixture. On the other hand, an item may be fixed yet remain a chattel, because there was no intention that the chattel should become part of the land, e.g. a tapestry fixed to a wall for display. In other words, there is plenty of scope for argument.

It is always possible to evade argument by special conditions in the contract. You could have a condition saying that the sale excludes the shrub roses, but includes the carpets and wardrobes. Fine, but this specific condition is of no use when the purchaser bitterly complains that Harry has taken the sundial from the garden. Was Harry justified? Was it a chattel or a fixture?

In its national protocol the Law Society encourages the use of a fixtures, fittings and contents form which lists in detail which items are, or are not, included in the sale. You will have sent this form to Harry for completion or have asked him to complete it at the initial interview. This completed form is then attached to the agreement and forms part of it (see special condition 4). Harry will spend a pleasant half-hour filling in the form, stating against each item listed in the form whether the sale includes it, or excludes it. The sundial? It is one of the items noted in the form (garden ornaments). So the dispute will be settled by reading the form to see if Harry said he would be leaving it, or taking it.

(n)   Special Condition 5

This offers alternatives. Harry is selling with vacant possession, so you will cross out the alternative statement that the sale is subject to existing tenancies.

(o)   Other Special Conditions

The facts do not seem to justify any other special conditions. The gaps in the agreement – e.g. remedies for late completion – are filled in by the standard conditions incorporated into the contract. Most of the standard conditions are mentioned in other chapters of this book.

Before practising the drafting of another agreement, we shall pause to consider the drafting of special conditions relating to the seller's title.

5.3   The Implied Promise as to Title

Although the seller's promise as to his title is the most important of the promises he gives in the contract, you will rarely see the promise expressed in the contract. The parties rely on the fact that the promise is *implied*.

The implied promise is that the seller has a good title to the freehold estate free from incumbrances. Clearly, if he cannot live up to this promise, it must be changed by an express condition in the agreement.

It is because of this promise in the contract that it is said that the seller has a duty to disclose latent defects in title. However, this duty of disclosure is perhaps better understood as a *precaution* of disclosure. If there is a flaw in the seller's title, and this is not disclosed to the purchaser before the contract is made, then inevitably the seller is breaking his promise as to title. The purchaser, on discovering the defect before completion, may be able to say that the breach is serious enough to discharge the contract, or may be able to claim a reduction in the purchase price by way of damages. If, however, the seller discloses the defect before the contract is made, the contractual promise is altered. If the defect is disclosed, the purchaser has, by implication, agreed to buy subject to it. The promise by the seller is now 'good title, free from incumbrances, with the exception of this particular matter which has been disclosed to the purchaser'. Disclosure cuts down the seller's promise as to title.

What follows will be easier to understand if you realise that a defect in title may consist of a third-party right enforceable against the land – for example, an easement, covenant or lease. The seller cannot then give title free from incumbrances. Alternatively, it may be what is known as a 'paper' defect – i.e. that there is something wrong with the documentary evidence of title. The deeds may not show that the seller owns the legal estate, or may show that his ownership could be challenged. He would not then have a good title.

What Must the Seller Disclose?

Unless the contract says otherwise, the answer is *'latent* defects in *title'*. So from this we can see that:

(a) *He need not disclose physical defects* There is no implied promise in the contract about the physical state of the property. This is why the purchaser should consider having the property surveyed before he decides to buy. However, a physical defect *may* give the purchaser a cause of action against the seller:

   (i) if before contract the seller states the property is free from physical defect, and the statement is untrue. The purchaser would have remedies for misrepresentation (see Chapter 20);
   (ii) if the contract *does* make an *express* promise about the physical state of the property;
   (iii) if the property being sold is a leasehold, rather than a freehold estate. The physical defect, if a breach of covenant in the lease, may also be a defect in title (see Chapter 16);
   (iv) if the seller has taken active steps to conceal a physical defect before contract. This may amount to fraud;
   (v) if the seller built the house and did it negligently (*Anns* v. *Merton London Borough Council* [1978] and see Defective Premises Act 1977).

(b) *The seller need not disclose patent defects in title* A patent defect has been defined by case law as a defect that is visible to the eye or can reasonably be inferred from something that is visible to the eye (*Yandle & Sons v. Sutton* [1922]. The logic of this is that as the land discloses the defect to the purchaser, there is no need for the seller to do it. A path across the property might mean that the private right of way along the path would be a patent defect. It was held in the Yandle case however, that a *public* right of way was not necessarily to be inferred from the existence of a pathway. Few defects will be patent. A defect in the paper title will always be latent as it will be discoverable only by looking at the deeds. A lease is a latent defect, even though the tenant is living on the property. In the case of unregistered title, s.24 of the Law of Property Act 1969 makes it clear that the fact that an incumbrance is registered as a land charge under the Land Charges Act 1972, does not make it into a patent defect.

(Do not allow yourself to become confused at this point. Remember we are talking about the responsibility of the seller to tell the purchaser about third-party rights. We are *not* discussing whether or not the rights will bind the purchaser on completion, when registration or occupation might be very relevant).

(c) *The seller need not disclose third-party rights that will not bind the purchaser on completion* They are not defects in title. If the seller is a trustee of land, he need not disclose the interests of the beneficiaries behind the trust, as he can, by conveying with another trustee, overreach them.

Another example would be an option to buy that has not, in unregistered title, been registered as a C(iv) land charge, or, in registered title, been protected by an entry on the seller's register. The non-registration will make the option void against the purchaser. The same would hold true of unprotected restrictive covenants, although in fact these would have to be mentioned in the contract if an indemnity covenant were required (see Chapter 12).

It should now be made clear that although generally the disclosure of the defect to the purchaser means that he has agreed to buy subject to it, this does, in fact, only apply to an irremovable defect. If a defect is removable – for example, as above, by the appointment of a second trustee – then the purchaser is entitled to assume that it will be removed. This is why it is the duty of the seller to ensure that all mortgages and other financial charges are paid off before completion, even though the purchaser knew of the charges before contract. If, in fact the sale is to be subject to the financial charges, there must be a special condition saying this. (Remember that if it is a financial charge in favour of a local authority, the contract may say that the sale is subject to it; see standard condition 3, discussed later).

Notice two further things about the duty of disclosure:

1. The seller is under a duty to disclose *all* incumbrances, even those he does not know exist. Remember the promise is freedom from *all* undisclosed incumbrances. Therefore, if the purchaser, before completion, discovers a third-party interest over the property which the seller has not told him about, the seller would, in the absence of a condition in the contract, be in breach of contract. It would be no excuse for the seller to say that the non-disclosure was due to his complete ignorance of the interest. The only way that he could escape liability would be to establish that the interest was a patent, rather than a latent, incumbrance (but notice the effect of standard condition 3, discussed later).
2. In unregistered title, the duty of disclosure covers all defects in the paper title, except a pre-root defect which the seller did not know about. The exception arises from s.45 of the Law of Property Act 1925, which is explained in Chapter 8.

5.4 When Do We Need to Alter the Implied Promise as to Title?

(a) When We are Not Selling the Freehold, But the Leasehold

It must be made clear that it is a leasehold estate that is being sold. The particulars will generally give details of the lease, and a copy of the lease will accompany the draft contract (see Chapter 16).

(b) When the Seller Does Not Have a Good Title to the Estate

The seller's promise that he has a good title is not a promise that the title is completely flawless, but that it is a title that will lead to quiet possession of the land, without any real threat of dispute or litigation.

If there is a defect in his title, the first thing for the seller to consider is putting his title into order. If the conveyance to him was void – for example, because it was not properly executed – he may be able to ask for a confirmatory conveyance. He may be able to trace a plan lost from a past deed, or to contact a past mortgagee to obtain a receipt that should have been previously endorsed on a redeemed mortgage.

However when faced with a defect in the paper title that cannot be put right, the last resort of the seller is a special condition which details the defect, and then says that the purchaser cannot raise any objection to the title on that ground. It is a last resort, because if the defect is serious, a purchaser will reject the draft agreement, and look for a different property to buy. However, if the defect is there, and cannot be put right, a special condition is the only answer to the problem. A reluctant purchaser might be tempted into the contract by a reduced price, or by arranging insurance against third-party claims.

A condition saying that a purchaser cannot object to some part of the title, or indeed saying that the purchaser cannot object to the title at all, is valid, but only *provided* that the seller is honest. He must disclose defects in the title either that he knows about or that he ought to know about, and then preclude the purchaser from objecting to the title (*Becker* v. *Partridge* [1966]). After such disclosure, the purchaser is bound by the contract, even if the seller's title is not just questionable but non-existent.

This problem of paper defects is peculiar to unregistered title. The only comparable points in registered title would be:

(i) the fact that the registered title is not absolute, but is possessory or qualified. The class of title should be detailed in the agreement, and a copy of the entries in the register will accompany the draft agreement. The purchaser can be prevented by a special condition from requiring any other evidence.

(ii) the possibility of someone having the right to apply for rectification of the register, e.g. a squatter who has been in adverse possession for over twelve years. This defect, being latent, would have to be disclosed. (Remember that the fact that an interest is overriding has nothing to do with the seller's duty to tell the purchaser about it.)

(c)   When the Seller's Land is Subject to Third-Party Rights (e.g. easements, restrictive covenants, options, etc.)

A special condition in the contract will state that the sale is subject to them. The purchaser, before accepting a term that says the sale is subject to a third-party right, will naturally want details of it, and if it was created by a document, will want a copy of that document. This will be supplied with the draft agreement.

5.5   The Effect of Standard Condition 3.1

Read this condition. How does it alter the position outlined in 5.3?

Condition 3.1.1 says that the seller is selling free from incumbrances. It then retreats from this general promise by saying that the sale is however subject to the incumbrances listed in 3.1.2.

Those listed in 3.1.2 are:

(a) Incumbrances mentioned in the agreement. Remember that when drafting Harry's agreement for sale we mentioned the right-of-way on the first page. The sale then became subject to the incumbrance. The incumbrance must be mentioned in the agreement if the sale is to be subject to it. If it is not mentioned, the sale is not subject to it, even though it is revealed by the evidence of title that accompanies the draft agreement.

(b) Incumbrances discoverable by inspection of the property before contract. This reflects the open contract rule about patent defects. However, when we were considering patent defects we saw that most defects in title are latent. The only safe thing for a seller to do is to mention in the contract a defect of which he knows and never to assume that it is a patent defect.

(c) Incumbrances that the seller does not and could not know about. You may remember that the *implied* promise is that there are *no* undisclosed incumbrances, and that it would be no defence for a seller to say that he did not disclose the incumbrance because he did not know it existed until the purchaser discovered it. Condition 3 alters this. The seller promises freedom only from incumbrances he knows about. So if an undisclosed incumbrance is discovered by the purchaser, the seller is not in breach of contract if the seller did not know of the incumbrance. The condition talks of those the seller 'does not and *could not* know about', so the seller must not only have been ignorant of the incumbrance when he entered into the contract, but must also have lacked the means of discovering the defect. If the defect were discoverable by the seller, e.g. by reading his own deeds or inspecting his own property, he is treated as knowing of it. It brings in the idea of constructive knowledge.

(d) Entries on any public register. 'Public register' is defined to exclude the register kept under the Land Charges Act 1972, the register of title kept under the Land Registration Act 1925, and entries of a company file kept at Companies House. Thus if there is a registered land charge (unregistered title) or a caution or notice (registered charge) affecting the property that is not disclosed in the agreement the seller will be in breach of contract.

(e) Public requirements. These are defined in condition 1.1.1 as 'any notice order or proposal given or made (whether before or after the date of the contract) by a body acting on statutory authority'. This means for example that the sale is subject to all local land charges. Condition 3.1.4. emphasises this by stating that the purchaser must bear the cost of complying with all public requirements, and must indemnify the seller against any liability arising from a public requirement.

5.6 Barring Requisitions

According to standard condition 4.1.1 the purchaser must raise requisitions on title within six working days after the date of the contract or the date of delivery of the evidence of title, whichever is the later. So it is still contemplated by the standard conditions that the purchaser can leave investigation of title until after the two parts of the agreement have been exchanged, and then object to the title because it is not a good title, or because it is subject to incumbrances not mentioned in the agreement but known to the seller.

If the seller wants to force the purchaser to investigate title before exchange he can alter the standard conditions to prevent the purchaser raising requisitions on the evidence of title supplied, once agreements are exchanged. In other words, the purchaser will contract to accept title as deduced pre-exchange.

A special condition such as this would not prevent a purchaser from objecting to the title on the ground of the concealment by the seller of a defect known to him (see 5.4 (b) and *Becker* v. *Partridge* [1966]) or because of a defect not revealed by the evidence of title supplied (Re *Haedicke* v. *Lipski*'s Contract [1901]).

5.7   Drafting a Contract for the Sale of an Unregistered Title

(a)   Introduction

While bearing all this in mind, attempt the drafting of an agreement for the sale of an unregistered freehold title. You are using the same form of agreement incorporating the standard conditions of sale. Your clients are Harry and Martha Hill. The estate agent's particulars and the information given by your clients disclose that the house is a large detached house, standing in two acres of ground. It is in a poor state of repair. There is a public footpath cutting across the far corner of the garden.

Imagine it is now 1998. You have the following deeds:

(i)   a deed dated 1940 conveying the freehold estate on sale, made between B and C as sellers and D as purchaser. It describes the property as being 'Blackacre, in the village of Little Hove and in the parish of St James the Vernacular, in the County of Wessex, as the same is bounded to the North by Mr Fitzgerald's property, to the West and South by the park paling of Lord Footscray, and to the East by the London to Folkstone Road'. It also says that Blackacre is more particularly described on the plan attached to a conveyance dated 1 April 1910 and made between A of the one part and B and C of the other part. It says that the property is conveyed subject to restrictive covenants contained in the 1910 deed. (You do not have a copy of this deed.) B and C are expressed to convey as trustees.

(ii)   A deed dated 1989, conveying the estate on sale from D to your clients. It describes the property simply as 'Blackacre, Lower Hove, Wessex'.

(iii)   A mortgage dated 1989 by your clients to the Champagne Building Society.

Notice that you do not have any search certificates against the names of the past estate owners. This means that you cannot be certain that there are not land charges against those names that may have been created by documents that you do not have in your possession.

A cautious solicitor would feel that he did not really know his clients' title without certificates of search, and might now make searches against the names of A, B, C, D, Harry and Martha. (It is certainly always worth thinking about making a search against your own client's name. This might reveal a class F registration (spouse's rights of occupation under Family Law Act 1996) and a C(i) or C(iii) (a mortgage unprotected by deposit of the deeds, i.e. a second mortgage). It is better to know about these before contract than after, when their existence may mean that your client is in breach of contract). If you are following the protocol, you must do these searches now, anyway, and the certificates should be sent to the purchaser as part of the pre-contract package (see section 1.4). You should have no difficulty in completing the first page of the agreement, apart, perhaps, from the particulars.

(b)   Particulars

In unregistered conveyancing, there is often a temptation simply to copy out a description from a title deed. In this case, it would be foolish to use the verbal description in the 1940 deed, as it is clearly now out of date. Also the 1940 deed describes the land by reference to a plan. The plan is lost. For that reason alone, you obviously cannot refer to the plan in the particulars of sale. Even if you had the plan, it would not necessarily form a good basis for the contract description. You would certainly need to confirm that the plan actually represents the present boundaries. In fact, if there is no doubt about where the present boundaries lie, there is unlikely to be any need for a plan to form part of the contract description. (A plan might be vital when a client is selling only part of his property. For example, he might be selling the end of his large garden to a developer. It is necessary to establish the new boundary and a plan is the only way to do it. Of course, the plan must be professionally prepared, and it will be used in the conveyance or transfer as well as in the agreement for sale). In our case, it is probably sufficient to describe the land as the freehold land known as Blackacre, Lower Hove, Wessex. (There is no *need* to add, 'and the house built on it' as the house is a fixture and forms part of the land.) The difficulty most often lies in checking that the title deeds are dealing with all the land that is *now* recognised as forming part of Blackacre. Boundaries move. (Look at the problem in the workshop section of Chapter 9.)

(c)   Root of Title/Title Number

You now have to state how title shall be deduced.

Here, of course, you are dealing with an unregistered title, so what you must do is specify the document with which your evidence of title will start, i.e. the root of title.

If an agreement for the sale of an unregistered title says nothing about the commencement of title, the rule is that the seller must start his evidence of title with a 'good root' at least 15 years old. (Again, do not get confused here. For both registered and unregistered title, the promise as to title is the same, i.e. that the seller has a good title to the freehold. Here, however, we are talking about the *evidence* that he must produce to substantiate that claim. As has been seen, in registered conveyancing, the evidence is the register of title. In unregistered conveyancing, the evidence comes usually from the past deeds.) A good root is a document which shows the legal and equitable interest passing from one owner to another, which identifies the land, and which does not itself make the title seem doubtful in any way. Both a conveyance on sale and a deed of gift can be good roots. A purchaser would probably *prefer* to find that the good root is a conveyance on sale, as the purchaser under that conveyance would have investigated the title before he bought. A donee might not have done this. However, if the contract is silent about the start of the title, the purchaser will have to accept a deed of gift as a root of title.

Usually, a contract will not be silent as to the start of the evidence of the title. It will specify the document that is to form the root. Usually, the seller will specify what would have been a good root anyway, and will choose a document that is at least fifteen years old. The reason is that if he proffers a document that is not a good root, or one that is immature, the purchaser may simply say that the condition in the draft agreement is unacceptable. There is a risk in a purchaser agreeing to accept evidence starting with a root less than fifteen years old. The risk is that the purchaser misses seeing a section of the title that he would otherwise see, and he may miss a name that he could otherwise search against in the Land Charges Registry.

To illustrate this, suppose that you, as purchaser's solicitor in 1998, see in the draft agreement a condition that title will be traced from a conveyance dated 1 May 1986 made between John Williams and Albert Black. You notice that the condition does not say whether the conveyance was on sale, or by way of a gift, and that the conveyance is only twelve years old.

If the agreement had not specified a root, you would have been entitled to one at least fifteen years old. Accepting a root only twelve years old does not mean that you are missing an investigation of three years of ownership. You might be missing considerably more. The conveyance by which John Williams obtained the property might be dated 1930, and it would have been from that that you could have traced title.

Before completion, you will be making a search at the Central Land Charges Registry against the names of past estate owners revealed by the abstract of title. By accepting an immature root, you cannot add the name of the person who conveyed the land to John Williams. If anything is registered against that name, for example, a land charge D(ii) because he (the person who sold to John) burdened the land with restrictive covenants when he bought it, you will take subject to the land charge, and you will have no right to compensation from the Chief Land Registrar (see Chapter 20).

Suppose the conveyance to John was dated 1920, and created restrictive covenants. Again you would take subject to these covenants, even though the later deed might make no mention of them. As they arose before 1926, the covenants are not registrable, but bind people who have actual or constructive notice of them. Your failure to see the 1920 conveyance, when under an open contract you would have been entitled to do so, fixes you with constructive notice of anything you would have discovered had you done so.

To return to the drafting of the Hills' agreement, which deed will you specify as the root of title? You know that the purchaser will object if you put the 1989 conveyance forward as a root, as it is not yet fifteen years old. What about the 1940 deed? It *is* fifteen years old. It does show the legal estate and equitable interest passing from B and C to D. (Although B and C, being trustees, may not themselves have *owned* all the equitable interest, they could still pass it to D, because of their powers of overreaching beneficiaries' claims.) It does not disclose anything suspicious about the title. However, it does not by itself describe the property. It refers to the 1910 plan for a better description. Most purchasers, seeing the description in the 1940 conveyance, would instantly demand a copy of the 1910 plan, on the basis that the description in the 1940 deed is inadequate without it. This point of view may not be correct, as the verbal description in the 1940 conveyance might well be a sufficient description, but the point in drafting an agreement for sale is to anticipate difficulties.

So, if you had a copy of the 1910 deed, you would have a choice. You could still state that the root of title is the 1940 deed, but supply a copy of the 1910 plan with the draft agreement. (Strictly speaking, you should supply a copy of the entire 1910 conveyance, so the purchaser can check if the plan is said to describe the land in detail, or merely provide a general identification.) Or, you could state that the 1910 conveyance is itself to be the root of title.

In this case, it would scarcely matter which course you adopted. It would have made a difference if there had been documents of title between 1910 and 1940 as they would not have to be abstracted if the root were the 1940 conveyance, but would have to be abstracted if it were the 1910 conveyance.

However, you do not have a copy of the 1910 conveyance. So nip objections in the bud. Say in the agreement that title will be traced from the 1940 deed, and that no copy of the plan on the 1910 conveyance can be supplied, and that the purchaser shall not be entitled to ask for it. There seems to be no need here for any clauses to be added on the second page.

Notice that nothing is said in the contract about the disrepair of the property. There is no duty on the seller to disclose physical defects, and standard condition 3.2.1 states that the purchaser accepts the property in the physical state it is in when the contract is made.

(d) Incumbrances

The public right-of-way must be mentioned here. Do not assume it is discoverable by inspection of the land.

You must also mention the 1910 restrictive covenants.

However, as soon as the purchaser sees a condition in the draft agreement saying that the sale is subject to the covenants, he will naturally demand a copy of the 1910 conveyance, to see what they are. We cannot supply him with a copy. The deed appears to have been lost forever. All we can do is to say in the contract that no copy of the covenants can be supplied, and that the purchaser can raise no requisition as to what the covenants are, nor as to whether or not they have been broken. (Faruqi v. English Real Estates Ltd [1979]).

Of course, this is a condition that may deter our prospective purchaser. However, there is nothing else we can do. The purchaser probably need not be unduly concerned with the existence of the covenants if he does not intend to change the existing use of the land. If our clients can confirm that no objection to the existing use has been made by neighbouring land-owners in the past, it is unlikely there will be one in the future. The purchaser should be concerned if he intends to develop the land – for example, pull down the house and build a block of flats. This might be breaking the covenants (which bind the purchaser in this case because of actual notice) and a furious neighbour who has the benefit of them may object. One solution for a purchaser who does want to buy the land is to insure against the risk of the covenants being enforced.

(e)   Title Guarantee

To complete the first page of the contract, you must decide what title guarantee your clients will promise. As they have lived in the property, they are probably safe to offer a full title guarantee (see Chapter 20).

5.8   Other Conditions that it Might be Necessary to Add to an Agreement for Sale

(a)   Deposit

Standard condition 2.2 provides for a 10 per cent deposit to be paid on exchange by the purchaser to the seller's solicitor who is to hold it as stake-holder. We have already considered the possibility that a purchaser might ask to pay a smaller deposit (see section 2.3). The point here is the capacity in which the deposit is held by the solicitor. A stakeholder holds a deposit as agent for both seller and purchaser, so cannot release it to either until the contract is discharged. Usually the contract will be discharged by the successful completion of the contract, when the deposit is released to the seller. It is possible for the contract to be discharged (i.e. terminated) by one party breaking the contract. If the breach is the purchaser's, the seller is entitled to call for the deposit to be forfeited to him. If it is the seller who has broken the contract, the purchaser can ask for the deposit to be returned to him. While the contract still exists, the deposit is frozen.

The exception to this is standard condition 2.2.2. This applies when the seller is buying another house. The seller would like to use the deposit paid on his sale to finance the deposit he must pay on his purchase. This is possible, as the condition provides that the deposit may be released to the seller to be used to buy another property in England or Wales for his residence. If the seller would like to have the use of the deposit before completion for some other purpose, the standard condition does not permit this. A special condition would have to be substituted saying the deposit is to be paid to the seller's solicitor as agent for the seller. This change is likely to prove unpopular with the purchaser. A deposit paid to a stakeholder is safe if the seller goes bankrupt, as the trustee in bankruptcy has no better right to the deposit than the seller, i.e. usually, only if and when the sale is completed. A deposit paid to an agent of the seller is not safe; it belongs to the seller. To recover it, a disappointed purchaser would have to prove in the bankruptcy. The only safeguard is that if a deposit is paid to a seller or seller's agent, the purchaser has a lien on the seller's land for its recovery. The lien is in the nature of an equitable charge, so the purchaser is a secured creditor. However, the lien offers no comfort if there are prior mortgages that exhaust the value of the property.

You must also consider the need for a special condition if the deposit is to be held by someone other than the seller's solicitor. A special condition must provide for this, and state in what capacity the deposit is to be held. It seems that a deposit paid on exchange of contracts to the seller's estate agent will be held by him as agent for the seller unless the contract says otherwise. (Note that 'solicitor' for the purpose of the standard conditions is defined to include a licensed conveyancer.)

At common law a stakeholder is entitled to keep any interest earned by the deposit. Higher standards are, however, expected of a solicitor. The Law Society insists that interest earned by a deposit should belong to the client, not the solicitor. (See the Law Society's Guide to Professional Conduct of Solicitors (7th Edition) Chapter 25, paragraph 15.) Standard condition 2.2.3 reflects this, as it provides that on completion the deposit is to be paid to the seller with 'accrued interest' (this term is defined in standard condition 1.1).

What if, as events turn out, the deposit has to be returned to the purchaser? The purchaser will then receive accrued interest paid by the seller – see standard condition 7.2.

(b)   Sale of Part

We have seen that if the seller is selling only part of his land, the drafting of the particulars will require care. He must also consider the grant and reservation of easements, and the giving or imposition of restrictive covenants. This topic and the effect of Standard Condition 3.4 are considered in Chapter 12.

(c)   The Need for an Indemnity Covenant

This is considered in Chapter 12.

(d) Sale Subject to an Existing Tenancy

If the land is to be sold subject to an existing tenancy, this should be stated in the special conditions, for example, 'the sale is subject to the weekly periodic tenancy of the top floor, the tenant being Mr Alex Brown'. A copy of the tenancy agreement should be supplied to the purchaser with the draft contract. The purchaser is then treated as entering into the contract with full knowledge and acceptance of the terms of the tenancy (condition 3.3.2).

The sale may be to the sitting tenant himself. If this is so, the tenancy will probably end on completion, as it will merge into the freehold that the purchaser has acquired. However, this is a matter for the purchaser. The contract will still say that the sale is subject to the purchaser's own tenancy, and that as he is the tenant, he is taken to buy with full notice of terms of the tenancy.

The purchaser must, of course, read the tenancy agreement. He must not lose sight of the fact that if it is a residential tenancy, the agreement will not in fact reflect all the rights of the tenant. These may be considerably increased by statute.

If the tenancy was created before 15 January 1989 it may be protected by the Rent Act. This Act gives the tenant considerable security of tenure, and may limit the amount of rent that can be recovered from him.

If the tenancy was created on or after 15 January 1989, the Housing Act 1988 (as amended) will apply, and the tenant may have some degree of security of tenure, but little rent protection.

Standard condition 3.3.2(e) emphasises that the purchaser must satisfy himself as to whether the tenancy is protected by either Act and as to what rent is legally recoverable.

(e) Sale of a Matrimonial Home when the Legal Estate is Owned by only One of the Spouses

This is dealt with in Chapter 11.

(f) Sale of a Leasehold Estate

Additional matters to be borne in mind when drafting a contract for the sale of a leasehold property are dealt with in Chapter 16.

(g) Absence of Title Deeds

If the title is unregistered, and the seller bases his title on adverse possession, or while having documentary evidence of his title does not have either the original or a marked copy of every title deed, he should alter standard condition 4.2.2 and 4.2.3.

5.9 Conditional Contracts

The seller and the purchaser may agree to the sale of the property, but 'subject to' some matter being first of all settled. This qualification can have different results:

(a) It may mean that there is no contract at all. The phrase 'subject to contract' nearly always has this effect.
(b) It may simply be one of the terms in a concluded contract. In this sense, it is possible to say that the contract is 'subject to' the purchaser paying the price, or 'subject to' the seller making good title. In *Property and Bloodstock Ltd* v. *Emerton* [1967], the contract was expressed to be subject to the seller obtaining his landlord's consent to the assignment of the lease. It was held that this was a promise by the seller as to title. It did not create a 'conditional contract' in the sense that the phrase is used in the next paragraph.
(c) It may create a conditional contract. This term is used here to mean a concluded contract, but one which cannot be enforced by either party until a condition is fulfilled. If the condition is not fulfilled within its time limit, both parties are released from the contract.

If the parties wish to create a conditional contract, they must make their intention clear, and must ensure that the condition is sufficiently certain.

A condition is void for uncertainty if it is impossible for the court to decide the circumstances in which it could be said to be fulfilled. If the condition is void, the contract is void. If the contract is to be conditional on planning permission, for example, the condition should give details of the permission being sought, and whether or not it will be fulfilled by an outline planning permission, or by one with conditions attached.

A contract subject to the results of a local land charge search and additional enquiries should say that it depends on the results being satisfactory to the purchaser or his solicitor acting reasonably. This is a standard that can be objectively tested by the court. (See *Janmohamad* v. *Hassam* (1976) and *Smith and Olley* v. *Townsend* [1949].)

5.10 Formalities for the Creation of a Contract for the Sale of Land

Nothing has been said as to the legal formalities until this late stage, because if the usual conveyancing procedures are followed, the formalities will inevitably be observed.

Section 2 of the Law of Property (Miscellaneous Provisions) Act 1989 states that a contract for the sale or other disposition of an interest in land must be in writing. The contract must incorporate all the terms which the parties have expressly agreed. It will incorporate the terms if it actually contains them or if it refers to some other document which contains them.

The contract must be signed by or on behalf of each party to the contract.

If, in the usual way, contracts are prepared in duplicate with a view to exchange, s.2 will be satisfied if *both* copies incorporate all the agreed terms, and if each party signs one copy, even though they sign different copies.

The result of s.2 is that there can no longer be an oral contract for the sale of land. Under the previous law (s.40 of the Law of Property Act 1925) an oral contract was unenforceable. Now, there can be no such thing as an oral contract.

Interest in land is defined to include an interest in the proceeds of sale of land – i.e. an equitable interest existing behind a trust of the legal estate.

Section 2 does not apply to a contract to grant a lease for a term not exceeding 3 years at best rent without a premium nor to a contract made at auction. At auction, the contract comes into existence at the fall of the auctioneer's hammer. Both seller and purchaser are in fact then invited to sign a written contract, but the contract exists without the writing.

Section 2 provides that the document must incorporate all the terms agreed between the parties, so that if one party can point out that a head of agreement is *not* contained in the written contract, the contract becomes void. One answer to this could be rectification of the contract on the ground that the written document by mistake does not express the true agreement of the parties (see *Joscelyne* v. *Nissen* [1970].)

The parties to the contract may wish to alter its terms. It has been held that any alteration must itself be in writing signed by both parties (*McCausland* v. *Duncan Lawrie Ltd* (1996)) So, if the alteration is oral, or is made by letters written by the parties' solicitors, the alteration will be void, and the contract will take effect as originally drawn.

Workshop

Attempt this problem yourself, then read the specimen solution at the end of the book.

Problem

(This problem is best attempted after you have read Chapter 11.)

You have been instructed to act for Ada Faulkener in the sale of her cottage. You have borrowed the title deeds from Doom Building Society, Ada's mortgagee. There is a memorandum on the conveyance to Ada to the effect that part of the garden was later sold by Ada to a neighbour in June 1980. You did not act for Ada then. You have taken the precaution of obtaining a land charges search against her name. The search reveals a D(ii), a C(i) and an F land charge registered against her name, all apparently affecting the cottage. None of the entries can be explained by the documents in your possession. What action will you need to take in respect of the matters disclosed by your search and when?

N.B. Exercises in drafting an agreement for sale are set at the end of Chapters 12 and 13.

6 Pre-contract Searches and Enquiries

6.1 Introduction

You now know that a seller has a duty either implied or expressed in the contract to disclose certain defects in his title to the purchaser. Much information which might affect the value or the enjoyment of the property, and make it unattractive to the purchaser is not within this duty of disclosure. He should seek out this information before contract. As the seller is not under a duty to disclose it, it is too late for a purchaser to discover it after the contract, as there will be no breach of contract to offer him a remedy.

The solicitor for the purchaser therefore always makes, or ensures that he has the results of, what are known as the 'usual' pre-contract searches and enquiries. They are called 'usual' because they are applicable to nearly every transaction. There are also 'unusual' searches which might have to be made because of the property's location. A purchaser's solicitor who fails to obtain the usual searches, and whatever other searches are considered necessary as a matter of good conveyancing practice, will have failed in his duty to his client.

6.2 The 'Usual' Searches and Enquiries

(a) Enquiries of the Seller (the Seller's Property Information Form)

Making the Enquiries   There have been until the introduction of the protocol and perhaps will continue to be, many standard lists of enquiries to be asked by the purchaser of the seller. At one time the Oyez form reigned supreme, but in recent years has been challenged by others. The number of questions grew steadily and the answers given by the seller's solicitor became increasingly non-committal and unhelpful. To quote from the Law Society's introduction to the protocol:

> if any one part of the conveyancing process over the past years has caused criticism within the profession it has been the use of ever-lengthening forms of enquiries before contract, some being a repeat of those included in the standard form and others being irrelevant to the particular transaction or relating to the structure or condition of the property.

The protocol documentation now includes what is called the 'Seller's Property Information Form'. Part I of this form is completed by the seller, and part II by the seller's solicitor. The form is then sent to the purchaser's solicitor as part of the pre-contract package. The form reads as a series of questions and answers. Why? To quote again from the Law Society:

> the property information form continues to be set out as replies to a series of standard questions. Since the seller's solicitor will be providing this information it might be seen as more logical at a future date to develop this as a simple statement of information without the question and answer format. However there are two reasons for retaining this. First it is a system with which the profession is familiar and secondly, it is hoped that even in those instances where for any reason the protocol is not being followed the buyer's solicitors will still use the property information form rather than revert to other forms for raising enquiries before contract.

The form is in the Appendix for you to read. Below are a few of the questions in Part I of the form.

(i) Question 4 asks if the property has the benefit of any guarantees. This might cover guarantees given after damp or timber treatment or in respect of double glazing. A purchaser should ensure that the benefit of the guarantees is expressly assigned to him on completion.

According to the protocol, if there are any such guarantees, the seller's solicitor should obtain copies of them and send them to the purchaser's solicitor with the property information form.

This enquiry may also reveal the fact that the house is protected by the National House Building Council's Scheme (known as 'Buildmark'). This scheme covers houses, bungalows, flats or maisonettes built by a builder or developer who is registered with the Council. The scheme protects a purchaser for ten years against the developer's failure to build the house properly and against structural defects. It is backed by insurance cover. The purchaser from the developer must ensure that he has the protection of the scheme and that he receives the necessary documentation, i.e. offer of cover form, the booklet that explains the scheme and the warranties that are given by the developer, and the 'ten year' notice, which is issued by the NHBC and which brings the scheme into operation. Any subsequent purchaser who buys while the ten year protection period is still running should ensure that the booklet and the ten year notice are handed over to him. The benefit of the scheme will pass to him without having to be expressly assigned.

(ii) Question 5 asks what services (e.g. gas and electricity) the property has and the routes taken by the pipes, wires, etc., and whether they have to cross anybody else's land to reach the property. The point of this is to investigate whether any necessary easements exist.

(iii) Question 8 asks the names and ages of any person in actual occupation of the land, and what legal or equitable interest such an occupier has. Having read Chapters 3 and 4 you know why a purchaser is concerned about anybody other than the seller occupying the land. The age of the occupier is relevant because it is suggested that if the occupier is so young that he cannot be considered as independent of his parent, the child is not in actual occupation for the purposes either of constructive notice, or s.70(i)(g) of the Land Registration Act 1925. An answer denying that anybody else is in occupation is usually accepted in practice, unless the purchaser knows better, but an untruthful denial by the seller that Uncle George is in occupation does not clear any interest that Uncle might have from the title, although there would be a cause of action against the seller. (This is elaborated in Chapter 11.)

(iv) Question 10 checks on compliance with planning requirements (see section 6.5).

Part II of the form that is completed by the seller's solicitor asks more technical questions, for example as to easements benefiting the property, the existence of overriding interests and as to who has the benefit of restrictive covenants burdening the land. The solicitor is also asked if the sale is dependent on the seller buying another property, and if so, whether he needs and has arranged a mortgage loan to finance the purchase. This is to check if there is likely to be a delay before the seller is in a position to exchange contracts. The seller's solicitor owes a duty of confidentiality towards his client, and must not reveal these details without his consent.

The protocol also recommends that the purchaser's solicitor tell the seller's solicitor about the position of the purchaser's own sale, and the progress of his mortgage arrangements to finance the purchase, but again only if the purchaser consents.

Having received the pre-contract 'package' the purchaser's solicitor may make additional enquiries but according to the protocol only those specific additional enquiries which are required to elucidate some point arising out of the documents submitted or which are relevant to the particular nature or location of the property or which the purchaser has expressly requested, but omitting any enquiry, including one about the structure of the building, which is capable of being ascertained by the purchaser's own enquiries or survey or personal inspection.

If the sale is of a leasehold property, the purchaser's solicitor must also be sent a completed 'additional property information form'. This is discussed in Chapter 15.

Replying to the enquiries   Imagine now that you are the seller's solicitor. The replies to the questions on both parts of the form are the seller's. You formulate and sign the replies to the questions in Part II of the form as his agent. An incorrect answer may mean that the seller can be held liable for misrepresentation (see Chapter 19).

If it is due to your carelessness that the answer is wrong, you will be liable to your own client for any loss you cause him. In *Sharneyford Supplies Ltd v. Edge (Barrington Black Austin & Co [a firm], third party)* [1987] an enquiry was raised as to the existence of tenancies. The solicitor for the seller, *without consulting his client*, said that the tenants had no security of tenure. The purchaser successfully sued the seller when the tenants were found to be irremovable, and the seller's solicitors were ordered to indemnify their client.

(b)   The Local Land Charge Search

Each district authority (or for Greater London, each London Borough or the Common Council of the City of London) maintains a register of local land charges affecting the land within its area. It is difficult to define a local land charge, except to say generally that it is something designated as a local land charge either by the Local Land Charges Act 1975 itself or by some other Act. They are matters affecting land that are public matters, rather than private ones, and are registrable either by the district authority itself, or some other statutory body. Their name is legion, but they include:

 (i) *Financial charges*   Examples would be charges to recover the cost of street works, or the cost of emergency repairs to unsafe buildings, or to recover some forms of improvement grant.
 (ii) *Planning matters*   These include conditions imposed after July 1977 on planning permissions, enforcement notices actually in force, tree preservation orders.
(iii) *The listing of buildings as being of special architectural or historic interest*   This listing restricts demolition and alteration of the building, and so can remove any development potential from the land (see *Amalgamated Investment and Property Co. Ltd* v. *John Walker & Sons Ltd* [1976]).

It is not clear to what extent the existence of a local land charge will constitute a defect in the seller's title. A financial charge and probably an order requiring demolition of the property will be a matter of title and therefore fall within the seller's duty of disclosure. (In this context, consider the case of *Rignall Developments Ltd* v. *Halil** [1987].) If a local land charge, or other local authority matter, is not a defect in title, it does not have to be disclosed. These rules are affected by the standard conditions. Consider again standard condition 3.

As many local land charges are not matters of title, and so not within the seller's duty of disclosure and as standard condition 3.1.2 makes the sale subject to all of them anyway, the purchaser will ask the authority to make a search of the local land charges register *before* he enters into the contract. The official search certificate will list any land charges registered at the date of the certificate, but the certificate is not conclusive nor does it give the purchaser any priority period. (See Local Land Charges Act 1975.) The purchaser will take subject to all charges in existence at the date of the search, whether revealed by the certificate or not, and subject to all charges coming into existence after the date of the search. What the certificate does do is give a limited right to compensation. A purchaser who relies on an official search certificate before entering into a contract can claim compensation if he is adversely affected by a land charge that existed at the date of the search but was not registered, or by a charge that was registered but was not disclosed by the search certificate. (A purchaser who relies on a *personal* search of the register can claim compensation only in respect of a local land charge that existed, but was not registered.)

To claim compensation the purchaser need not have ordered or made the search himself. It is sufficient if he or his solicitor had notice of the contents of the search certificate before exchange of contracts (s.10 of the Local Land Charges Act 1975). That is why, if a seller is anxious to speed matters on, he could make the search and include it in the pre-contract package. Notice, however, that no compensation is payable in respect of local land charges that come into existence after the date of the search, so certificates become increasingly useless with age.

It is usually pointless for a purchaser to repeat a local land charge search after contract but before completion, because, if any new matter has arisen, standard condition 3 will have thrown the burden of it onto the purchaser anyway. However, the purchaser's intended mortgagee may ask for the search to be repeated, and may withdraw or reduce the loan if anything adverse is discovered.

It is because the certificate is not conclusive that Enquiry 3 on the property information form asks the seller if he has received any notices or communications from the local authority or other statutory body.

(c)   The Enquiries of the District Authority

The district authority will know much that will not be revealed by the local land charge search, for the simple reason that the information is not registrable as a land charge. This information can be extracted from the authority by raising enquiries. There is a standard form of enquiries, approved by local authorities. The form is divided into two parts. The first contains questions that are always answered by the authority. The authority will only answer those questions in the second part which the enquirer has ticked, and for which he has paid an extra fee. The enquirer may also add further questions of his own devising, but the authority can refuse to answer these.

Examples of Part I Enquiries

(i) *Roads*   The Authority is asked if the road and paths giving access to the property are maintained at the public expense, and if not, whether the authority has passed a resolution to make up the roads, etc., at the cost of the frontagers. It is also asked if it has entered into any outstanding agreement relating to the adoption of any such road or path, and if any such agreement is supported by a bond.

If you are buying a house that is reached by a road that is not maintained by the local authority, the following problems arise;

(aa) *Easements*   Does the house have easements over the road, so that the purchaser will have the right to walk and, if relevant, drive over the road without relying on someone's permission?

(bb) *Maintenance*   At the moment, is anyone under an obligation to repair the roadway? The answer may be 'no', as the owner of land subject to a right of way does not generally have a duty to keep the way in repair. Sometimes, there is an agreement between the people who use or own the road to maintain it.

(cc) *Future expenses*   Has the local highway authority resolved to 'make up' the road? Under the Highways Act 1980, the local authority can pass a resolution to 'make up' a road not previously maintained at the public expense. When the road has been repaired to a suitable standard it is 'adopted' by the authority and from then on will be maintained out of public funds. This sounds like good news to the owners of houses reached by the road. The drawback, however, is that the authority can apportion the cost of the work that brings the road up to standard in the first place among the owners and occupiers of premises which have a boundary adjoining the road. This can involve an owner in considerable expense. The owner (and his successors) can be sued for debt by the authority, and in addition the amount due is a charge on the property and registrable as a land charge.

A developer building estate roads will normally enter into an agreement with the authority under s.38 of the 1980 Act. The developer promises the authority to build the estate roads to a certain standard. The authority agrees that once the roads are completed, it will adopt them. The developer may be selling the completed houses before the roads are adopted. If he breaks the agreement, and does not build the roads to the required standard, the authority can do the work, and charge the houseowners. So the purchaser might find that he is having to pay a substantial amount towards the creation of the road. The developer may have covenanted in the conveyance to the purchaser that he would complete the roads, but the problem has probably arisen in the first place because of the developer's insolvency.

To avoid the problem, the s.38 agreement is supported by a bond, given by, for example, an insurance company. The insurance company promises the authority that if the developer does not make up the roads, the cost of the authority doing it will be paid by the insurers. This does not remove all risk, as if the sum promised under the bond is insufficient to cover the costs of the roads, there will again be a charge to the frontagers.

So a purchaser of a house on a new estate where the roads have not yet been adopted, will want to be satisfied as to the existence of the s.38 agreement, and as to the existence and adequacy of the bond.

(ii) *Sewers*   The authority is asked if the property is served by a sewer maintained at the public expense.

In the case of a new building estate, there may be an agreement between the developer and the authority under s.104 Water Industry Act 1991, similar to the agreement under the Highways Act. The authority is asked to disclose the existence of any such agreement and supporting bond.

(iii) *Various planning matters*   designed to gauge the authority's planning intentions for the area.

(d)   Search in the Index Map, and Parcels Index

This search is usually only relevant when the purchase is of unregistered title. It is made at the District Land Registry that serves the area in which the land lies. It will reveal:

(i) whether the title is unregistered, or registered. It is apparently possible for it to be forgotten that a title has been registered, and for subsequent owners to deal with it as if it were unregistered. None of these unregistered dealings will have passed the legal estate. It may also warn the purchaser that there has been a previous sale of part of the land dealt with by the title deeds.

(ii) if the title is registered, the title number, and whether the title is freehold or leasehold.

(iii) any caution against first registration. This can be lodged by anyone who fears that an application for first registration will prejudice his rights over the land. The effect of the caution is that the Registrar must inform the cautioner of any application for first registration. The cautioner then has an opportunity of claiming that his interest should be noted on the register, or perhaps that registration should not take place at all.

(iv) any pending application for first registration.

(e)   A Search in the Land Charges Register against the Seller's Name

This will only be relevant when buying an unregistered title. It is not essential to make a search of the central land charges registry before contract, as any registered land charge should be disclosed by the seller. (See section

5.3 of this book, s.24 of the Law of Property Act 1969 and standard condition 3.)

If the seller's solicitor is following the protocol, he will have made a search against the seller's name and against the names of the other estate owners revealed by the evidence of title and have supplied the certificate of search to the purchaser as part of the pre-contract package (see section 1.4).

If the protocol is not being followed, and the purchaser's solicitor is not given evidence of title before exchange of contracts, it is impossible to make the search pre-contract. The purchaser's solicitor does not know the names of the estate owners. However, in these circumstances, a cautious purchaser might consider making a search before contract against the seller's name. It might give early warning of his bankruptcy, or the registration of a Class F land charge. The purchaser might then decide that the least troublesome thing to do would be to buy a different house.

(f) Company Search

If the seller is a limited company, a cautious buyer may decide to make a company search now. Alternatively, this search may be delayed until before completion.

(g) Inspection of the Property

The property should be inspected before contract

  (i) to look for physical defects (see section 6.4).
 (ii) to look for patent defects in title (see section 5.3).
(iii) to look for dangerous occupiers (see sections 3.16 and 4.4).

This inspection is far more likely to be done by the purchaser, than by his solicitor.

6.3 The 'Unusual' Searches

There are searches that will be made only for certain localities (for example, areas where minerals have been won, or limestone or salt extracted) or particular problems (for example, where the land is cut by a rail line or a canal). Details of the searches required can be found in specialised textbooks on conveyancing searches.

One of the more common is the search made when buying land in a coal-mining area. The search is made with the Coal Authority. Information will be obtained as to the whereabouts of existing workings, plans for new workings, whether a claim for subsidence has already been made, and whether any compensation has been paid. The Law Society has published a directory setting out the areas where a coal-mining report should be obtained.

Another search worth mentioning is the commons registration search. Each County Council maintains a register of common land in its area, and a search in this register might reveal that rights of common exist over the property. The search should be made if land has never been built on, or only recently built on, particularly if it is in open country or on the edge of a village.

6.4   The Survey

As the contract promises nothing about the physical condition of the property, it is sensible for a purchaser to have the property surveyed before he agrees to buy it. He can instruct a surveyor to carry out a full structural survey. Even this cannot guarantee the complete soundness of the property, as inspection is limited by problems of access to floorboards, rafters, etc. The cost of a full survey is currently about £600 for a three-bedroomed house, and surprisingly few purchasers commission one. A cheaper alternative is a house-buyer's report, which comments on the condition and value of the property, and lists visible serious defects.

If the purchaser is borrowing money to buy the house, the prospective lender will instruct a surveyor to carry out a valuation report. The Royal Institute of Chartered Surveyors stresses that this is not a survey. Its purpose is only to value the property to decide if it offers sufficient security for the loan. Some lenders let the purchaser see this report, others do not, although in all cases it is the purchaser who pays for the inspection to be carried out. Well over three-quarters of house-buyers rely on this report alone. Whether or not the purchaser sees the report, he assumes that the lender would not lend unless the report was satisfactory. It is now settled that on the purchase of a 'modest' house, the lender's surveyor owes a duty of care to the purchaser and cannot protect himself from liability for negligence by a disclaimer of responsibility. (See *Smith* v. *Eric S. Bush, Harris* v. *Wyre Forest District Council* [1990]*.)

6.5   Town and Country Planning

Planning matters feature in the preliminary enquiries, the local land charge search and the additional enquiries of the district authority. For this reason a brief outline of planning law is given here.

(a)   Development of Land

Note: A reference in this section to 'the Act' is a reference to the Town & Country Planning Act 1990 as amended.

Planning permission is needed for the development of land (s.57 of the Act). Development is defined as:

(i) the carrying out of building engineering, mining or other operations in, on, over or under the land;
(ii) the making of any material change of use of any buildings or other land (s.55 of the Act).

Buildings and other operations   It is clearly development to build a house or to extend an existing house. It is development to add a garage, or a potting shed. It is development (because it is an engineering operation) to make an access way from the house to the highway.

However, the Act expressly provides that internal or external improvements or alterations to a building are not development if they do not materially affect its external appearance (s.57(2) of the Act).

Change of use   A *material* change of use is development. As a guideline, a change in the kind of use will be material, but a change in the degree of use will only be material if it is substantial. Thus, to change the use of a house from residential to a business use would require planning permission. For an owner-occupier of a house to take in a lodger would not be a material change of use, but for the owner-occupier to turn his house into a boarding-house probably would be.

It is specifically provided that it is a material change of use if a single house is used as two or more separate dwellings. This point is of concern to a purchaser of a flat created by the conversion of a house (s.55(3) of the Act).

It is not a material change of use if a building or land within the curtilage of a dwelling house is used for any purpose incidental to the enjoyment of the house as such. That is why no permission is needed to start using an existing outhouse as a garage. (Remember it *is* development to build a new garage.)

To assist in the decision of whether or not a change of use is material, there exists the Town and County Planning (Use Classes) Order 1987. This specifies various classes of use. For example, Class A1 is use for the purpose of most sorts of shop. Class A2 is use for the provision of financial or professional services to the visiting public (e.g. the offices of Building Societies, or banks). Class B1 is use as an office other than as in Class A2.

A change of use from one use to another is not development, provided that both uses are within the same class. A change from use in one class to a use outside that class may be development. It will depend on whether the change is considered to be material. For example, to change from a clothes shop to a grocery store will not be development, as both uses are within class A1. Similarly, a change from an accountant's office to a solicitor's office will not need permission, as both uses are within Class B1. A change from a clothes shop to use as a branch office of a Building Society would need permission as it would be a change of use that would be considered material.

(b) Applying for Planning Permission

(i) If you are not sure whether the proposed activity constitutes development, you can apply to the local planning authority for a decision on the point (s.64 of the Act).

(ii) If planning permission is needed, you must consider whether express permission is needed, or if the General Permitted Development Order can be relied on.

(iii) The Town and Country Planning (General Permitted Development) Order 1995 itself gives planning permission for certain developments. For example:

Part I Class A – development within the curtilage of a dwelling-house This includes enlarging a house, (subject to limitations on the volume and the height of the extension), and building a new garage (subject to limitation on size and situation). If the proposed development is outside the limitations imposed by the order, express planning permission will be needed. Class I also permits the erection of greenhouses, sheds, chicken-houses, etc.

Part II Class A – minor operations These include erecting fences (subject to limits on height) or painting the outside of the building.

Before relying on permission given by the general development order, you must check if an 'article 4' direction exists. This will be revealed by the additional enquiries of the local authority. The local planning authority can direct that all or any of the permissions granted by the General Development Order shall not apply to the whole or part of its area. For example, the authority may withdraw the permission granted for the erection of chicken-sheds. Anybody wanting to build one would then have to apply for express planning permission.

(iv) If express planning permission is needed, the application must be accompanied by detailed plans. If the applicant does not own the land, he must certify that he has notified every owner of the land. 'Owner' includes an owner of the freehold, and anyone owning a lease with seven or more years to run. (s.66 of the Act).

(v) If you propose to build on land and want to check that there is no objection in *principle* to the development, you can apply for outline planning permission. This commits the authority to allowing that type of development while allowing it to control any matter that is expressly reserved in the outline permission for later approval, such as the exact siting of the buildings, or their appearance. This procedure avoids the delay and expense of preparing detailed plans, when the application in fact never had any chance of success. (Outline planning permission is not available for a proposed change of use.)

(vi) The planning authority must give written notice of its decision within 2 months of the application. If the decision is not made within this period, the applicant can, if he wishes, treat the failure to give a decision as a refusal of permission, and appeal to the Secretary of State (ss.78 and 79 of the Act).

Once a planning permission has been given, it enures for the benefit of the land, so that a purchaser of land will acquire the benefit of existing permissions. That is why one often sees a house advertised for sale with the benefit of a planning permission. However, a purchaser must remember that planning permissions do lapse (see next paragraph).

Duration of Planning Permission

(i) A planning permission is subject to a condition that development will be begun within five years of the date of the grant or whatever period is specified by the authority. If development is not begun, the permission lapses.

(ii) An outline planning permission is subject to a condition that application for approval of the reserved matters be made within three years of the grant of the outline permission and that development be begun within either five years of the grant of the outline planning permission, or two years of the approval of the reserved matter, whichever is the later (Sections 91 and 92 of the Act).

(c)   Enforcement of Planning Control

(i) If development is carried out without permission, or is in breach of a condition imposed on the planning permission, the local planning authority can issue an enforcement notice (s.172 of the Act). The notice has to be served on the owner and on the occupier of the land, and any person who has a property interest in the land which might be affected by the notice. The notice is first of all issued; it may then be served not more than 28 days after its issue. It will specify a date on which it is to become effective, and this must be at least 28 days from the date of service.

(ii) Time limits for service

These time limits have been changed by provisions of the Planning and Compensation Act 1991 which came into effect on 27th July 1992. The new time limits are as follows:

(aa) If the breach consists of an unauthorised building, mining or other operation, the notice must be served within four years of the breach.

The four-year rule also applies to an unauthorised change of use *from* any building to use as a single dwelling-house.

(bb) If the breach consists of any other unauthorised change of use or is a breach of a condition attached to a planning permission, the notice must be served within ten years of the breach.

Once the time limit for service of an enforcement notice has passed, it is possible to obtain a certificate of lawfulness of the existing use or development. This certificate will not only establish that the development or change of use is immune from an enforcement notice, it will also amount to a grant of planning permission so that the development or new use becomes legal.

(iii) Failure to comply with an enforcement notice is a criminal offence, and there is liability for fines and other severe financial penalties. In addition, if the enforcement notice specifies steps such as the demolition of an unauthorised building, or reinstatement of the land to its previous condition the authority can enter onto the land and do the work itself, recovering the expense from the owner of the land (s.178 of the Act). This means that if a purchaser buys land that had, say, a garage built on it by the seller without planning permission, it is the purchaser (as the current owner) who will have to pay the authority's costs of demolition. The purchaser will be able to recover this expense from the seller (see s.178 of the Act). The authority cannot enter onto land to force discontinuance of an unauthorised use.

(d)   Planning and the Property Information Form

Having digested all this, we can return to the property information form and question 10 on it.

The protocol requires the seller's solicitor to send with the property information form all planning decisions and building regulation approvals that the seller possesses. If he is buying a new house, the purchaser will want a copy of the planning permission for its erection. He will also want a copy of the building regulations consent given by the Local Authority under the Public Health Acts.

Even if he is not the first purchaser of the house, he will want to see a copy of the planning permission, as he will want to check not only that permission was obtained to build the house, but also if conditions were imposed on the permission, and if these conditions have been broken within the previous ten years. He will also require details of any further building on the land, or any improvements or alterations made in the previous four years. You can now see why the enquiries as to building works are confined to this period. If a garage was built or altered more than four years ago, no enforcement notice can be served.

If the purchaser is hoping to acquire the benefit of an existing permission for future development, he will want to check that the permission has not lapsed, or will not shortly lapse. If the purchaser intends to enlarge the house under the authority of the general development order, he must ask for details of any previous extensions carried out. The point is that the *original* volume of the house can only be increased within specified limits, so previous additions may already have exhausted those limits. If the house has been in existence since 1 July 1948, any enlargement since that date will be relevant.

(e) Building Regulation Approval

Apart from planning permission, a purchaser of a new house, or of a house recently substantially altered, needs evidence that the Building Regulations were met. The purpose of these regulations is to ensure that houses are safe and provide a decent living standard. Major alterations must comply with them, but smaller improvements such as conservatories are exempt.

Building Regulations approval must be obtained from the local authority. The current regulations are the Building Regulations 1991 (as amended).

Case Notes

Smith v. Eric S. Bush [1990] 1AC 831, [1989] 2 All ER 514 [1989] 2 WLR 790

In this case, a firm of surveyors was instructed by a building society to carry out a visual inspection of a house and to report on its value. The surveyor noticed that two chimney-breasts had been removed, but failed to check if the chimneys had been left adequately supported. His report said that the house needed no essential repairs.

The application form for the mortgage loan and the valuation report both contained a disclaimer of liability for the report's accuracy, both on behalf of the building society and the firm of surveyors. The borrower, Mrs Smith, was warned that the report was not a full survey, and that she should seek independent advice. The building society supplied her with a copy of the report, and in reliance on it she bought the house. One chimney collapsed. She sued the surveyors for negligence, who relied on the disclaimer.

Harris v. Wyre Forest District Council [1990] 1AC 831, [1989] 2 All ER 514 [1989] 2 WLR 790

In this case, the Council lent money to Mr and Mrs Harris. It instructed one of its employees to value the property. The application form for the mortgage said that the valuation report was confidential, and that the Council accepted no responsibility for the value or condition of the house by reason of the report. The Council's valuer recommended minor repairs. Three years later it was discovered that the house suffered from serious structural faults. The Harrises sued the Council, as being responsible for the negligence of its employee. They had not seen the report, but had assumed, when the Council continued with the loan, that it must have been favourable.

It was held in both cases that a valuer instructed by a prospective lender to carry out a valuation of a house at the 'bottom end' of the market to decide if it offered sufficient security for the loan, owed a duty of care to the borrower to exercise reasonable skill and care in carrying out the valuation, if he realised that the borrower would probably buy the house in reliance on the valuation, without having an independent survey.

It was stressed that this principle applied on the purchase of a 'modest home', when there was great pressure on a purchaser to rely on the valuation report, because he might be unable to afford a second survey fee. Lord Griffiths expressly reserved his position in respect of valuations of industrial property, large blocks of flats, and very expensive houses. In these cases, it would be more reasonable to expect the purchaser to arrange his own full structural survey.

In neither of these two cases had the surveyor exercised reasonable skill and care as, although only a limited appraisal was expected, it was by a skilled professional person, and each surveyor was guilty of an error which the average surveyor would not have made.

It is possible for a surveyor to disclaim liability for negligence, but the disclaimer would be ineffective under s.2(2) of the Unfair Contract Terms Act 1977 unless it was fair and reasonable to allow reliance on it, under s.11(3) of the Act. Since a surveyor was a professional person, whose services were in fact paid for by the borrower, it would not be fair and reasonable for him to rely on a disclaimer. Also, the disclaimer was unfair in that it was imposed on a person who had no power to object to it.

Rignall Developments Ltd v. Halil [1987] 3 WLR 394

The property was subject to a local land charge. It was a financial charge to recover an improvement grant made by the district authority. The seller knew that this charge existed. The property was sold by auction. One of the conditions of sale was that the purchaser was deemed to have made local searches and enquiries and that the property was sold subject to anything that might be revealed thereby.

After contract, the purchaser learned of the charge, and refused to complete. The seller argued that the condition in the contract prevented the purchaser from objecting to the charge. However, the validity of the condition depended on the seller disclosing any matter she knew of, and as she had not disclosed the charge she could not rely on the condition (see section 5.4). It was, therefore, her duty to remove the charge by paying the local authority.

It was argued as that s.198 of the Law of Property Act 1925 says that registration of a charge amounts to actual notice for all purposes, registration was equivalent to disclosure. (You will remember that this argument could not have been used had it been a *central* land charge, but s.24 of the Law of Property Act 1969 does not apply to local land charges.)

It was held that where there was such a condition, and the seller knew of the charge, s.198 could not discharge her duty of expressly disclosing the existence of the charge.

Workshop

Attempt these problems yourself, then read the specimen solutions at the end of the book.

Problem 1

Your client tells you that he has signed a written agreement to buy 'Fools Paradise', a freehold house at the price of £90 000. He shows you a copy of the agreement. It incorporates the standard conditions. He entered into the contract without having made or seen any local land charge search certificate or enquiries of the local authority. He has now discovered that the house is burdened with a financial charge in respect of the cost of road works prior to the adoption of the road on which the house fronts. The charge existed before he signed the agreement, but he tells you he knew nothing of it. Advise him.

Problem 2

You have been consulted by Mr David Jones who proposes to purchase a semi-detached house which was built sixteen years ago on a small private residential estate. The house occupies a comer site on the edge of the estate and the side road is a private unmade road. Mr Jones is particularly attracted to this house because the present owner built a very large garage five years ago at the bottom of the garden and fronting onto the side road. Since that time he has been using the garage for repairing motor vehicles and Mr Jones wishes to do the same. The present owner has said that he has been using the garage for this business since it was built although he admits that he did not get planning permission either to build the garage or to use it for business purposes.

(a) Explain the issues, other than planning matters, with which you will be concerned in your perusal of the agreement for sale, the property information form, the searches and the evidence of title, in the particular circumstances of this case.
(b) Can the Local Planning Authority require the garage to be demolished?
(c) If the garage is not demolished, can the Local Planning Authority prevent its continued use for business purposes?

(This question is based on one in the Law Society Summer paper 1983.)

Problem 3

Joan is thinking of buying a house, but she would need to build an extension to provide a bedroom for her elderly mother. The seller's solicitor has provided her with the pre-contract package in accordance with the protocol.

1. Will she need planning permission for the extension?
2. If she does need express planning permission, when should she apply for it?

7 Deducing and Investigating a Freehold Registered Title

7.1 Deduction of Title

As we have seen, the seller promises in the contract that he has a good title to the freehold estate, free from incumbrances (other than those, if standard condition 3 applies, mentioned in the agreement or of which the seller was ignorant). At some stage the seller must prove that he does indeed have that title. He must 'deduce' his title, i.e. give evidence of it. Traditionally title was deduced after contract. If the seller's solicitor is following the protocol, title will be deduced *with* the draft contract.

So we are now considering what evidence of title the seller must produce, if he is contracting to sell a registered freehold title.

7.2 Section 110(1) of the Land Registration Act 1925

In the case of a registered title, s.110 of the Land Registration Act 1925 stipulates that the seller *must* supply the purchaser with

- a copy of the entries on the register;
- a copy of the filed plan;
- copies or abstracts of documents noted on the register of title.

Note

(a) S.110 only requires the seller to provide *a* copy of the entries on the register. So the seller could merely photocopy the contents of his land certificate. This would provide the purchaser with details of the register of title as at the date when the land certificate was last brought up to date with the register. This date is printed inside the cover of the certificate, and the purchaser would need to be told this date, for the purpose of his pre-completion search.

Alternatively, the seller can provide the purchaser with an office copy of the register, filed plan, etc. (and this is made obligatory by standard condition 4.2.1). Office copies are obtained from the District Land Registry. They are dated and are as admissible in evidence as to the state of the register at that date as is the register itself.

It is preferable for the seller's solicitor to obtain *up-to-date* office copy entries for his own sake. He might be caught out if he relies on the land certificate when drafting the contract. A caution, and a notice protecting a spouse's rights under the Family Law Act 1996 can be entered on the register without the Land Certificate being put on deposit at the Registry, and so will not appear on the Land Certificate.

(b) Subsection (1) of s.110 cannot be altered by the contract. These documents *must* be supplied by the seller.

7.3 Section 110(2) of the Land Registration Act 1925

This provides that the seller must provide 'copies, abstracts and evidence (if any)' in respect of matters as to which the register is not conclusive. However, s.110(2) *can* be altered by contract.

Remember that the register is not conclusive:

(a) as to overriding interests. If the seller knows of an overriding interest, the effect of condition 3 is that the sale is only subject to the interest if it is mentioned in the agreement. The purchaser would at the draft agreement stage have been given whatever documentary evidence existed, and may have been prevented by a special condition in the agreement from requiring any other evidence.
(b) in the case of a possessory title, as to matters affecting the pre-registration title. The seller may have no evidence as to this title, and again a contractual condition would prevent the purchaser from asking for any.
(c) in the case of a leasehold title, as to the provisions of the lease and in the case of a good leasehold title, as to the validity of the lease. The points are dealt with in Chapter 15.

7.4 Investigation of Title

The protocol requires the copies of the register, etc., to be sent to the purchaser with the draft agreement, so some of the matters dealt with below would in fact have been dealt with before the purchaser decided to enter into the contract.

Suppose that as the purchaser's solicitor, you have the office copy entries and filed plan in front of you. Read them.

(a) The Property Register and Filed Plan

(i) Check the title number, estate and description of the property against the contract details. Care will be needed if there have already been sales of part of the land originally comprised in the title. The property register will indicate that part of the land has been sold off, and the filed plan will have been amended. Check that the seller is not contracting to sell land he has already transferred to someone else.

(ii) Check any reference to appurtenant rights. If the property register includes an appurtenant right, such as an easement, as part of the description of the property, you can be certain that the easement exists. The registration indicates ownership of the easement just as it indicates ownership of the estate to which it is appurtenant. If the register merely says that right is 'claimed' by the proprietor or that a deed 'purports' to grant the easement, the register is not conclusive as to its existence. The existence of the easement should be proved by the proprietor, unless the contract says otherwise.

(b)   The Proprietorship Register

(i) Check that the seller is the person who is registered as proprietor. Suppose he is not? The solution may be that:

    (aa) the seller is the personal representative of the dead registered proprietor (see Chapter 10).

    (bb) the seller is the trustee in bankruptcy of the registered proprietor (see section 9.10).

    (cc) the seller is a trustee, who has been appointed, but who has not been registered as proprietor (see Chapter 11).

However, the solution may be that the seller has contracted to sell a legal estate that is in fact vested in someone else.

The principle here is that a seller shows good title only by establishing that he owns the legal estate, or that the legal estate is owned by someone who can be *compelled* by the seller to convey it to the purchaser. This is illustrated by the case of *Elliott* v. *Pierson* [1948] in which it was held that the seller had proved a good title to the freehold when he established that it was owned by a limited company which he controlled. If he had not had control of the company he would not have made good title, even if the company had been willing to convey to the purchaser. This would not have created any difficulty if the purchaser had been equally willing to accept a conveyance by the company, but the flaw in the seller's title would have given a reluctant purchaser the opportunity to treat the contract as discharged.

(ii) Look for restrictions. Either the seller must have the restriction removed before completion, or he must comply with it. Otherwise, the transfer to the purchaser will not be registered.

(iii) Cautions. If a caution is discovered on the register, do not accept an explanation of why the protected interest is in fact void, and so could not be asserted against the purchaser. Insist that the caution must be removed from the register before your client enters into the contract.

(c)   The Charges Register

(i) Are there any entries on the charges register of incumbrances that are not mentioned in the agreement?

(ii) Registered charges. Unless the contract expressly says otherwise, a purchaser is entitled to a title free from any mortgage. There are two usual methods by which a registered charge can be removed from the register.

(aa) *through its redemption* – i.e. the loan is repaid. The seller will be using part of the purchase price to pay off the mortgage. In the case of registered title the evidence that the mortgage loan has been repaid is Land Registry form DS1 executed by the mortgagee.

In an ideal world, this form would be handed to the purchaser on completion. However, some banks and building societies refuse to seal a document discharging a mortgage in advance of payment, so it is not available at completion. The solicitor acting for the purchaser is often prepared to accept what are called 'the usual undertakings' from the solicitor acting for the mortgagee, who will usually also be the seller's solicitor. The undertakings are guarded in form, because the solicitor will only undertake to do things that are within his own control. So he will not undertake that form DS1 will be executed. He will only undertake that he will forward the money necessary for redemption to the mortgagee, and that if and when the form is sent by the mortgagee to him, he will send it on to the purchaser.

The purchaser accepts these undertakings, because it causes too much fuss and delay to object to an established practice. However, a purchaser does not have to accept the undertakings, and should not do so if there is a possibility that the execution of form DS1 might be delayed. The undertakings should not be accepted, for instance, if the mortgagee is a private person. A building society does not die, or go on an extended holiday. A private mortgagee might. Form DS1 must be available at completion.

An undertaking should only be accepted from a solicitor or licenced conveyancer. If the seller is acting for himself, an undertaking from him should not be accepted, and the form DS1 should be available at completion.

If part of the land in the title is being transferred, and the mortgagee is releasing only the part being transferred from his mortgage, Land Registry form DS3 will be used instead of form DS1. Form DS3 will say that the mortgage is discharged as regards the part of the land identified by the plan accompanying the form. This plan would also be executed by the mortgagee.

(bb) *through being 'overreached'*. The proprietor of a registered charge has a statutory power of sale. (s.101 of the Law of Property Act 1925 and s.34 of the Land Registration Act 1925).
The power arises when, under the terms of the mortgage, the money is due and owing. This means that someone purchasing from a registered chargee must read the mortgage. He may, in an old-fashioned mortgage, find a promise to repay on a specified date, usually six months from the date of the mortgage. It is on this date that the money is technically due, and the power arises. Other mortgages may say that the money is repayable on demand (in which case evidence is needed that the mortgagee has requested repayment), or that the money is deemed to be due as from the date of the mortgage. The only check that a purchaser need make is that the power exists and has arisen. The power should only be used by the mortgagee when it has become exercisable. It may become exercisable under s.103 of the Law of Property Act 1925 (because of failure to repay capital, pay interest, or because of a breach of a provision in the mortgage) or under the terms of the mortgage. Some mortgages exclude s.103 and specify the defaults on which the power of sale becomes exercisable, or even say that the power becomes exercisable without default as from the date of the mortgage. Whatever the mortgage may say, this question of exercisability is an internal matter between the mortgagee and mortgagor (s.104 of the Law of Property Act 1925). Someone purchasing from the mortgagee need not enquire as to whether the power of sale is exercisable, and will get a good title from the mortgagee even if it is not. (However, it is said that a purchaser who learns that the power of sale is not exercisable should not complete, as he will not get a good title.)
Equally, a mortgagee when selling must take reasonable precautions to obtain the true market value at the time of sale. Failure in this duty to the mortgagor will not invalidate the sale to a purchaser who is innocent of fraud or collusion. The mortgagor must sue the mortgagee for damages.
The power is to sell the mortgagor's legal estate, free from the mortgage of the mortgagee who is selling and from any mortgage later in priority. These mortgages cease to be claims against the land and become instead claims against the purchase money paid to the mortgagee who sold. The mortgages are not cleared from the title through their redemption, so the purchaser will not receive forms DS1 in respect of them. Even if the purchase price is not enough to repay the mortgages, the purchaser takes free of them. They no longer affect the land. Therefore, a purchaser from the proprietor of the first registered charge will receive on completion a transfer signed by the mortgagee, and the mortgagee's

charge certificate. When the transfer is registered, all registered charges will be cancelled.

A mortgagee has no power to overreach a mortgage which has priority over his own. Therefore, if the seller is the proprietor of say, the second registered charge, there is a choice. The sale must either be subject to the first mortgage (unlikely) or the mortgagee who is selling will redeem the first mortgage.

(d) Overriding Interests

These, of course, will not be discovered from looking at the entries on the register. Any known to the seller should have been disclosed in the agreement. If any overriding interest not disclosed by the agreement and known to the seller is discovered before completion, the seller has broken his contract. (This is assuming standard condition 3 applies to the contract.)

A transfer signed by the seller's attorney   This is discussed in 9.5.

7.5   The Pre-Completion Search: Form 94

This is the final step in the investigation of the seller's title.

The purchaser has evidence of the state of the title up to a certain date. If he was given office copy entries, it is the date of the office copies. If he was given a copy of the entries in the Land Certificate, it is the date that the certificate was last officially brought up to date with the register.

The object of the pre-completion search is to bring the purchaser's information up to date. The search form (Land Registry form 94A if a purchase of all the land in the title, 94B if a purchase of only part) consists in essence of an enquiry addressed to the Land Registrar, as to whether any adverse entry has been made on the register since one of the two dates mentioned above.

On receipt of the search form, the Registry will issue an official search certificate, saying whether or not adverse entries have been entered on the register since the date specified in the search form. This official search certificate gives a purchaser a priority period of 30 working days (i.e. excluding weekends and bank holidays) the first day of which is the date of delivery of the search at the Registry. Any entry made on the register during this period is postponed to the purchase, provided the purchase is completed, and an application to register the purchaser's title is delivered to the registry, before the period expires. So a purchaser is protected against last-minute registrations made after the date of his search.

It is important to apply for registration before the period expires, as otherwise anything that was being postponed to the purchase (e.g. an application to enter a caution) will cease to be postponed, so that when the purchaser does eventually apply for registration, the registration will be subject to it.

The priority period cannot be extended by another search. The second search will simply give a different priority period, and can only postpone applications made after the second search, but not ones made after the first search but before the second.

Subject to this limitation, a second search is worth making. It will give the second priority period, and will also reveal if an adverse entry has been put on the register since the date of the first search.

The priority period protects a purchaser. 'Purchaser' includes a prospective mortgagee or tenant. A search made by a prospective transferee acquires a priority period for the transferee, but not for the transferee's mortgagee. A search by the prospective mortgagee, however, does give a priority period both to the mortgagee and to the transferee. In other words, if Jane is the solicitor both for Bill, who is buying the house, and for the Larkshill Building Society which is lending Bill the money to do it, Jane will make only one search, on behalf of the Building Society. The priority period given by the search will protect both Bill and the Society against last-minute entries on the register, provided the application to register the transfer and the mortgage is delivered to the registry before the 30 days expire. (This is the effect of the Land Registration (Official Searches) Rules 1993).

A search certificate is not conclusive in favour of the purchaser, so if it is wrong (for example, if it fails to reveal an adverse entry) the purchaser will take subject to the entry. He will, however, be able to claim compensation from the registrar (s.83(3) of the Land Registration Act 1925).

The search can be made by post by telephone, by fax and in some cases by direct computer link to the Registry.

7.6   Other Pre-Completion Searches

(a)   At the Companies Registry

If the registered proprietor is a limited company, it appears unnecessary to search the company file at the Companies Registry.

(i) *Fixed charges* A fixed charge will not bind the purchaser unless protected by an entry on the register of the title at HM Land Registry, even though it is registered at the Companies Registry (s.60(1) of the Land Registration Act 1925).

(ii) *Floating charges* A floating charge will not bind a purchaser unless protected by an entry on the register of title. If it is so protected, the purchaser will need to obtain a certificate of non-crystallisation signed by the company secretary, or, preferably, by the owner of the floating charge. This certificate should be dated as at the date of completion.

(iii) *Winding up* A company that has been wound up, or is in the process of being wound up by the court, will have lost its powers of disposition. The winding-up proceedings could be discovered by a search of the company file.

However, it is generally considered that a purchaser will get a good title despite the winding-up. One reason is that while the company is still in the course of being wound up, the general principle will apply that a registered proprietor may be assumed to have full powers of disposal unless there is an entry on the register to the contrary. Another reason is that once the purchaser is registered as proprietor he will own the legal estate by virtue of statutory vesting, even though the selling company had no power to dispose of it.

It therefore seems that a purchaser from a company may rely on the register of title.

(b)   A Bankruptcy Search in the Land Charges Registry Against the Name of the Purchaser

This search has nothing whatsoever to do with the investigation of the seller's title, but is added to the list of pre-completion searches for the sake of completeness.

If the solicitor for the purchaser is also acting for the purchaser's mortgagee, it is his duty, as the mortgagee's solicitor, to discover if the purchaser is, or is about to become, insolvent. This can be done by making a search against the purchaser's name at the Land Charges Registry, to see if there is a PA(B) or WO(B) registered (see sections 4.5(a) and (b)). This is not a title search, and it has nothing to do with the seller's ownership of the property being sold. It is a status search, to prevent the mortgagee lending money to a bankrupt. It is done by sending to the Land Charges Registry a search form K16, which asks the Registrar to search only for bankruptcy entries against the names listed.

Of course, this search is not necessary if the loan is not to the purchaser of a registered title, but to the existing registered proprietor. In the latter case, entries as to the bankruptcy of the proprietor will appear on the register of title, and will be revealed by the Land Registry Search.

Workshop

Attempt this problem yourself, then read the specimen solution at the end of the book.

Problem

You are acting for William and Mary Thompson, who are buying a freehold dwelling-house, number 34 Holly Avenue, at the price of £34 000. They are obtaining an advance of £30 000 from the Best Building Society (for whom you act) by way of an endowment mortgage. The seller is the Z Finance Company Ltd, which is selling as second mortgagee free from incumbrances, the first mortgagee being the Y Building Society.

List the documents you will send to the Best Building Society after completion.

8 Deduction of Unregistered Title

8.1 Form of Evidence

In the case of an unregistered title, a seller deduces his title by providing evidence of what his title deeds say. At one time, he would have sent the purchaser an abstract of the deeds. This amounted to a précis of their contents, prepared in a stylised form. Nowadays, the simplest method of letting a purchaser know the contents of deeds is by sending him photocopies of them. The photocopy deeds must be accompanied by an epitome i.e. a chronological index of the accompanying deeds. The epitome should state whether each original deed will itself be available on completion, and whether it will be handed over then to the purchaser. In this book, 'abstract' is used to mean both the traditional abstract and the epitome.

8.2 What Deeds and Other Documents Should be Abstracted?

The abstract will start with the deed that the purchaser is entitled to see as the root of title. Usually there will have been a term in the contract specifying what deed this is to be. If not, the document must be one that is a good root of title at least 15 years old (see section 5.8(e)). The abstract may start with an earlier document in circumstances in which the purchaser is entitled to see a pre-root deed (see section 8.3(e)). Having started with the root, the abstract must then give details of every deed, document or event that passes the legal estate from owner to owner, and eventually to the seller. Notice again that he must establish either that he owns the legal estate, or that it is owned by someone who can be compelled by him to convey it to the purchaser. This has been discussed in the context of registered title in section 7.4(b).

8.3 Which are Not Abstracted?

(a) An abstract should not contain *information about equitable or other interests that will be overreached by the sale,* and so will not affect the purchaser. So, for example, on a sale by trustees of land the purchaser need not be given information about the interests of the beneficiaries. On a sale by a mortgagee, the purchaser need not be given details of mortgages later in priority to that of the seller's.

(b) *A lease that has expired by effluxion of time* For example, if a lease was granted in 1987 for ten years, and the tenant left at the end of the term in 1997, the purchaser need not be given a copy of that lease. If the lease ended by any other means, the purchaser should be given whatever information is available to prove its termination, so if the tenant surrendered the lease in 1993, the purchaser should see a copy of the lease, and of the deed of surrender.

(c) *Birth, death or marriage certificates* These are matters of public record, and the strict rule is that if a purchaser wants a copy he can get one for himself. What the purchaser must be given is the information he needs to do this, e.g. the date of the marriage. In fact, if the seller has these certificates, it would be churlish of him to refuse the purchaser a copy.

(d) Strictly, *equitable mortgages should be abstracted*, so that the purchaser can check on their redemption. Remember though, that an equitable mortgage can be created with little formality. So equitable mortgages are not usually abstracted if they have in fact been paid off. If however, an equitable mortgage has been protected by the registration of a C(iii) land charge, the registration should be cancelled, otherwise the purchaser is alerted to the existence of the mortgage, and will need evidence of repayment of the loan.

Any legal mortgage created after the root of title should be abstracted, together with any relevant vacating receipt.

A legal mortgage created before the root of title, but discharged at a date after the date of the root of title should be abstracted, together with any vacating receipt. If it was not redeemed or otherwise discharged until after the date of the root of title, it is part of the post-root title, no matter when it was created.

A legal mortgage created and discharged earlier than the date of the root of title need not be abstracted.

(e) *Pre-root deeds and documents* Generally, a purchaser has no right to see any deeds or documents that are dated earlier than the root of title.

Section 45 of the Law of Property Act provides that 'a purchaser shall not:

(i) require the production, or any abstract or copy of any deed, will or other document, dated or made before the time prescribed by law, or stipulated, for the commencement of the title, . . . ;

(ii) require any information or make any requisition, objection or enquiry, with respect to any such deed, will or document, or the title prior to that time . . .'.

This section prohibits the purchaser from making any objection to the soundness of the pre-root title. It is as if there were an express term in the contract itself preventing the purchaser from raising requisitions on title. We have seen that any such contractual stipulation is valid only if the seller has shown good faith, i.e. has revealed to the purchaser any defect he knows about or ought to know about (see section 5.4). The same is true of the s.45 interdiction. So the purchaser can object to the pre-root title if he establishes the existence of a defect that was known to the seller at the time of contract and not disclosed. For this reason, a seller cannot use the section to escape his duty of disclosure. Any pre-root defect known to the seller should be expressly disclosed, and the purchaser expressly prohibited from raising a requisition in respect of it. Further, an incumbrance that is still enforceable is a matter of the post-root title, even though created pre-root.

There are four exceptions to s.45, when a purchaser can insist on seeing a pre-root document. The first three are laid down by s.45.

(i) a purchaser can see a power of attorney, no matter what its date, if it authorised the execution of a document that is part of the title;

(ii) a purchaser can see a document no matter what its date which created an interest or obligation which still subsists, if one of the documents on the title conveys the land subject to the interest;

(iii) a purchaser can see a document which creates a trust, if one of the documents on the title disposes of the land by reference to that trust. This does not however apply to a trust which creates equitable interests that are cleared from the title by being overreached.

(iv) the fourth exception comes not from s.45 but from the definition of a good root, i.e. that it must describe the property that is being conveyed. If the root of title describes the property it is conveying by a reference to a description in an earlier deed, or to a plan in an earlier deed, it is possible that a purchaser can either insist on a copy of the deed being produced, or can claim that the root of title is not a good root, as not containing an adequate description.

These rights of a purchaser can be removed by a special condition in the contract, with the exception of the pre-root power of attorney. Section 125(2) of the Law of Property Act 1925 makes it impossible for the purchaser's right to any power of attorney affecting his title to be excluded by the contract.

(f) *Past land charge search certificates* These are not documents of title, and the purchaser is not entitled to the results of past searches. However, if the seller has any, it is courteous to send copies to the purchaser, as it may save him from repeating searches against the names of past estate owners. The protocol requires the seller's solicitor to provide a certificate of search against 'appropriate' names which must mean the names of all the estate owners revealed by the abstract.

8.4 Verification of the Abstract

The abstract or epitome is only *prima facie* evidence of the seller's ownership of the property. The abstract might be inaccurate, omit vital documents or memoranda, or, of course, be a complete fabrication. Either at or before completion the purchaser must see the original deeds.

If the seller will be retaining the title deeds, it is usual for the purchaser's solicitor to 'mark' the abstract (or the copy deeds, in the case of an epitome) i.e. to write on it the fact that it has been examined against the original, and that the abstract is correct. This statement is signed by the solicitor, who adds the date, and sometimes the place where the examination was made. In later transactions the marked abstract or marked deeds may be acceptable as evidence of title, without recourse to the original deeds. However, a solicitor who relies on a marked abstract or marked copies which then turn out to be inaccurate, might be accused of negligence. (The protocol requires the seller's solicitor to mark any copy or abstract of a deed that will not be given to the purchaser on completion before sending the copy or abstract as part of the pre-contract package.)

8.5   Retention by the Seller of Deeds at Completion

On completion, a seller must generally hand to the purchaser all title deeds in his control. The seller can, however, retain the title deeds if he is also retaining part of the land to which they relate (s.45(9) of the Law of Property Act 1925). In such a case the purchaser should:

(a) mark the abstract as examined against the original deeds (if not already done);
(b) ensure that a memorandum of sale of part is endorsed on the conveyance to the seller;
(c) ensure that the conveyance to him contains an acknowledgement and undertaking in respect of the retained deeds.

It will often be wise for a seller of part to retain a copy of the conveyance to the purchaser with his deeds. It will identify exactly what part was sold and disclose any easements or covenants given by the purchaser in favour of the retained land.

Workshop

Attempt this problem yourself, then read the specimen solution at the end of the book.

Problem

You are acting for Patrick O'Connor who is selling his freehold house. It is 1998. You have the documents listed below:

1. 4 July 1970 – a conveyance on sale from A to B, said to be subject to covenants contained in a deed dated 1950.

2. 4 July 1970 – a mortgage given by B to the Foundation Building Society, with a receipt endorsed on it dated 30 September 1973 executed by the Society.
3. 6 July 1970 – a lease by B to T for 40 years.
4. 20 September 1973 – land charges search against A, B and O'Connor.
5. 30 September 1973 – a conveyance on sale from B to O'Connor, subject to the 1950 covenants.
6. 30 September 1973 – a mortgage given by O'Connor to the Roof Building Society.
7. 9 February 1975 – a surrender of lease by T to O'Connor.

(a) When you are drafting the agreement for sale, which document will you specify as the root of title?
(b) What documents will you abstract when deducing title to the purchaser?

9 Investigating an Unregistered Title

9.1 Introduction

When investigating an unregistered title, we are looking for a flaw in the soundness of the seller's claim to own the legal estate, and for any third-party right that will bind the purchaser after completion but to which the sale has not been made subject by the contract. This is easier said than done.

It does not matter for present purposes whether we are investigating the title before exchange of contracts or after. In the former case we will ask for any defect to be put right before we agree to buy; in the latter case we shall raise a requisition on the basis that the seller has not proved that he has the title promised in the contract. Of course, if we agree by a special condition in the contract to accept the title as deduced, we must investigate the title before exchange of contracts, as our power to object to the title after contract will be limited (see Chapter 5).

We will start by considering the basic points of the root of title, the stamping of the title deeds, the identification of the property, execution of the deed, and the 'missing link'.

Suppose we are acting for Paula Prentiss, who is contracting to buy the freehold of Sandy Cottage from Ian Lane, and that it is 1998.

We receive an epitome of title, accompanied by the photocopies of two documents.

9.2 The First Document of Title

The first document is a deed of conveyance on sale dated 3 June 1971, and this deed is now going to be considered.

(a) The Root of Title

If the contract does not specify what document is to be the root of title, we will consider our right to have title traced from a good root at least 15 years old, and we will check that this conveyance satisfies the definition of a good root (see section 5.8(e)). Our contract doubtless specifies from what document title is to be traced, so the question as to whether this document is adequate as a root was considered before accepting the contractual condition. We will be wary of any condition compelling us to trace title from an immature root. The 1971 conveyance appears to be a good root, and is, of course, over 15 years old.

(b) Stamping

(i) If the 1971 deed is not properly stamped, this is a defect in the seller's title. A document that is not properly stamped cannot be produced in court, and a title that cannot be defended in court is not a good title. If the deed is not properly stamped, we shall insist that the seller have it stamped. (We can do this even though there is a condition in the contract saying that no objection can be raised to an insufficiency of stamps, as the condition is void, by virtue of s.117 of the Stamp Act 1891).

As the conveyance is on sale, we would expect to see the 'particulars delivered' stamp. We also need to check that the conveyance bears the correct *ad valorem* stamps. The difficulty is that the thresholds for stamp duty have changed over the years, as have the rates of duty. At times, rates of stamp duty have been graded, so the certificate of value (see section 2.17) was used not only to claim total exemption from duty, but also to claim a reduced rate, e.g. 0.5 per cent rather than 2 per cent. So it is possible for a conveyance to have a certificate of value and also *ad valorem* stamps. Details of past rates of duty should be kept to hand, so that the stamping of past conveyances and other documents can be checked.

One thing must always be wrong, namely the absence from a conveyance on sale of both a certificate of value and *ad valorem* stamps. Total exemption from *ad valorem* stamp duty could only ever be claimed through a certificate of value. If the conveyance contained no certificate, *ad valorem* duty was payable at the then full rate, no matter how low the consideration.

(ii) *A note about particular documents* In the past, not only conveyances on sale had to be stamped *ad valorem*. A deed of gift was also liable, the duty being calculated on the value of the land. A certificate of value could be used to claim a nil or a reduced rate. The deed had to be sent into the Stamp Office for the duty to be adjudicated, so the deed should bear a blue adjudication stamp. A deed of gift made on or after 25 March 1985 was liable for a 50p deed stamp. A deed of gift made after 30 April 1987 bears no stamp duty, provided it is certificated (see section 2.17).

An assent under seal was liable for a 50p deed stamp if made before 25 March 1985.

Mortgages and vacating receipts (with the exception of a building society receipt) were liable to stamp duty if made before 1 August 1971.

(c)   The Parties to It

Suppose the seller in the 1971 deed is John Smith, and the purchaser is Alice Hardy. John is a mystery to us and will remain so. We may never know how he obtained the legal estate, as that can only be revealed by investigating the pre-root title.

(d)   The Parcels Clause

We are hoping to establish that the land conveyed in the 1971 deed did include the land that Ian has contracted to sell to our client. Under an open contract, the seller must prove that the property he has contracted to sell is the same as that being dealt with by the title deeds. This obligation does not appear to be altered by the standard conditions, although condition 4.3.1 absolves the seller from having to prove the exact boundaries of the property or the ownership of the boundary fences.

The proof usually comes merely from the description in the deed, i.e. that it says it is conveying Sandy Cottage. If the deed does not make it clear that it is dealing with Sandy Cottage, further evidence is needed, for example, a declaration from Ian that the land has been occupied since 1971 under the authority of the title deeds without challenge from anyone.

(e)   Incumbrances

Reading the parcels clause in the 1971 conveyance might reveal the reservation of an easement not disclosed in the agreement but known to the seller. Reading the habendum might disclose incumbrances already existing before 1971 but not mentioned in the agreement.

(f)   Execution of the Deed

The formalities for execution of a deed by an individual changed on 31 July 1990 when s.1 of the Law of Property (Miscellaneous Provisions) Act 1989 came into force. The new formalities are set out in Chapter 14, where the drafting of a deed is considered. The old formalities are set out here, as they remain important when checking the due execution of a past title deed.

A deed executed before s.1 of the 1989 Act came into effect had to be signed and sealed by its maker, and delivered as his deed (s.73 of the Law of Property Act 1925). If these formalities were not observed, the document was not a deed, and could not create or convey a legal estate (s.52 of the Law of Property Act 1925).

We are unlikely to query the authenticity of a signature on a deed. In theory we could ask Ian to provide evidence that what purports to be John Smith's signature is indeed that very thing. In practice we would not do that. Anyway, in respect of the 1971 deed, any requisition by us would be countered by Ian quoting the rule that a deed or document 20 years old proves itself, provided it is produced from proper custody and there are no suspicious circumstances. A suspicious circumstance would be a startling difference between two signatures both purporting to be that of John.

Section 73 did also require a seal. The days of personal seals are long past, and a seal became only a red wafer disc to be obtained from any law stationer. However, it was still essential that a seal be on the conveyance *before* the maker signed. So if the 1971 conveyance does not bear a seal, evidence is needed that a seal was in position at the time of execution. If a seal was never there, nor anything such as a printed circle which might have served as a seal, then the document is not a deed, and could not have conveyed the legal estate (see *First National Securities* v. *Jones* [1978]; and *TCB Ltd* v. *Gray* [1986]).

The delivery of a deed is a matter of intention. A deed is delivered when it is signed by the maker with the intention that he shall be bound by it. If a person signs and seals a deed, it is inferred from this that the deed is also delivered, so we will not call on Ian for evidence that John delivered the deed.

Remember, the above paragraphs set out the old rules for execution of a deed. The present rules are set out in Chapter 14.

9.3 The Second Document of Title

We now turn to the second and final document of title. This is a conveyance on sale dated 1 March 1987.

(a) We again check stamping.

(b) We again consider the parties, looking particularly for the 'missing link'. If in 1971 the property was conveyed to Alice Hardy, we expect to see Alice Hardy conveying it in 1987 to Ian Lane. Suppose for the sake of argument, that we find that the seller in the 1987 deed is, in fact, Christopher Camp. We need an explanation. Perhaps Alice had died, and Christopher was her personal representative. If so, we would ask for a copy of the grant of representation, identifying Christopher as executor or administrator, and would turn to Chapter 10. Alternatively Alice might have gone bankrupt, and Christopher was the trustee in bankruptcy, in which case we would ask to see a copy of the bankruptcy order and the certificate of appointment of Christopher as trustee.

If the ownership of the legal estate had not passed to Christopher by operation of law, then it must have passed by conveyance. In the absence of such a conveyance, the title is bad. The legal estate remained in Alice, and only she had power to convey it to Ian. To put his title right, Ian must either procure a conveyance by Alice to himself, or prove to us that he can compel Alice to convey the property directly to our client (see sections 7.4(b)).

(c)   The Parcels Clause

We expect to see a description similar to that in the 1971 deed, or at least linked to it. For example, the 1971 deed might talk about 'Farmer Giles's 10-acre field', but (we hope) also refer to an annexed plan which shows that the field covered the site of what is now Sandy Cottage. The 1987 deed may talk about Sandy Cottage forming part of the land 'conveyed by the 1971 deed'.

(d)   Incumbrances

We are again looking to see if the 1987 deed created new incumbrances not disclosed in the agreement. There now follows a list of diverse points to be considered on investigating a title. The list is not complete, and must be read in conjunction with Chapters 10, 11 and 12.

9.4   Execution of a Deed by a Company

Again, the formalities for the execution of a deed by a company changed on 31 July 1990, but this time by virtue of s.130 of the Companies Act 1989, brought into force on that day. **The present formalities are set out in Chapter 14**. The previous formalities are set out here.

If a conveyance was executed by a limited company, the execution was valid if the conveyance was executed in accordance with the company's articles of association. If the company's articles incorporated Table A of the Companies Act 1985, its articles provided for a deed to be executed by the affixing of the company seal by the authority of the directors in the presence of a director and the secretary, or the presence of two directors.

By virtue of s.74 of the Law of Property Act 1925, if the company seal had been affixed in the presence of the secretary and director, the deed was deemed to have been duly executed, even if in fact the articles demanded different formalities. Further, a purchaser could assume that the deed had been executed so as to satisfy s.74 if there was on the deed a seal that purported to be the company seal, and signatures that purported to be that of secretary and director. So a purchaser could take these matters at face value.

It follows from s.74 that the company was bound by its deed executed in accordance with the section, even though the seal was affixed without the authority of a resolution from the board of directors (*D'Silva* v. *Lister House Development Limited* [1971] Ch 17 [1970] 1 All ER 858).

9.5 Execution of a Document by an Attorney

(a) Power of Attorney

A seller who will, for example, be out of the country when the sale of his property is to be arranged, may authorise someone else to sign all the necessary documents on his behalf. The authority is called a power of attorney. We will call the seller, who confers the power, the principal, and we will call the person on whom the power is conferred, the attorney.

(b) Scope of the Power

A purchaser, before accepting a conveyance or transfer signed by the seller's attorney, must consider whether the attorney has the necessary authority under the terms of the power to sign the conveyance. This is decided by reading the power, and seeing what acts it does authorise.

A power may be specific, i.e. may authorise the attorney to do only those things which are enumerated in the power. A power 'to do all things, and execute all documents connected with the sale of 10 Cherry Avenue' is clearly useless if an attorney seeks to establish his authority to execute a mortgage of 10 Cherry Avenue.

Alternatively, a power may be general. The power may say simply that the attorney is appointed in accordance with s.10 of the Powers of Attorney Act 1971. This confers on the attorney authority to do on behalf of his principal anything that can lawfully be done through an attorney. So this attorney can execute a mortgage or conveyance of 10 Cherry Avenue, or of anything else that the seller owns beneficially. (Section 10 does not apply to any function which the principal has as a trustee or personal representative.)

(c) Revocation of the Power

The purchaser must also consider the possibility that the power had been revoked before the attorney executed the deed. Most powers of attorney are given solely because the principal is not able himself to sign the documents. The attorney has no proprietary interest in the land that is to be conveyed. This type of administrative power can be revoked by the principal at any time. It is also automatically revoked by the death of the principal, or by his bankruptcy or mental incapacity.

By contrast, the attorney may have an interest in the property to be conveyed, and the power might have been given to protect that interest. An example would be a power of attorney given to an equitable mortgagee authorising him to execute a legal mortgage in his own favour. This type of power is called a security power, and can be made irrevocable. Section 4(1) of the Powers of Attorney Act 1971 provides that if a power of attorney is *expressed* to be irrevocable and is given to protect a proprietary interest of the attorney, then so long as the attorney has that interest the power is not revoked by any event, nor can it be withdrawn by the principal unless the attorney consents.

(d)   Protection for the Purchaser from the Attorney

But for the 1971 Act (and earlier Acts) the rule would be that if the power had been revoked before the attorney executed the conveyance or transfer, the conveyance would be void. Section 5 of the Powers of Attorney Act protects the person dealing with the attorney from the possibility of previous revocation of the power. It provides that even if the power has been revoked, the transaction by the attorney is nevertheless valid, provided that the person dealing with the attorney (i.e. the purchaser from the principal) did not know of the revocation. So it is not the fact of revocation that matters, so much as whether or not the purchaser from the principal *knew* of the revocation. (It must be remembered that knowledge of a revoking event – for example, the death of the principal – amounts to knowledge of the effect of that event, i.e. the consequent revocation of the power.)

Section 5 also provides that if the power is *expressed* to be irrevocable and is *expressed* to be given by way of security, the person dealing with the attorney is entitled to assume that the power can only be revoked with the consent of the attorney. Knowledge of the donor's death would in such a case be irrelevant. The person dealing with the attorney does not receive this protection if he knows that the power was not in fact given by way of security. The Powers of Attorney Act 1971 applies to all powers of attorney whenever created but only to transactions completed by the attorney on or after 1 October 1971. For the validity of transactions completed before that date, the effect of ss.123–128 of the Law of Property Act 1925 must be considered.

(e)   Evidence of the Power

On completion, the attorney will not part with the deed creating the power if it is a general power, or if it authorises any disposition other than that to the purchaser. What he will give the purchaser is a facsimile copy (e.g. a photocopy) certified by the solicitor as being an accurate copy. This copy is then conclusive evidence of the contents of the original power (s.3(1) Powers of Attorney Act 1971). This means that anyone later investigating title need never see the original power; he need only see the copy, which has been handed from purchaser to purchaser with the title deeds.

(f)   Protection of Later Purchasers

We can see that the validity of the title that the attorney gives to the person dealing with him may depend on whether or not that person knew of a revocation of the power. There are two occasions when it is conclusively presumed in favour of any subsequent purchaser that the person dealing with the attorney did not know of a revocation.

One is where the transaction between the attorney and the person dealing with the attorney is completed within 12 months of the date of the power. The other is where the person dealing with the attorney makes a statutory declaration before or within 3 months of the subsequent purchase that he did not at the material time know of the revocation of the power (s.5(4) of the 1971 Act).

Example An example might help. Vimto has agreed to sell Blackacre to Pedro. Vimto gives his solicitor, Alexis, a power of attorney to execute a deed of conveyance and to complete the transaction.

Alexis executes the deed and completes on 1 October 1989. The conveyance to Pedro will be valid unless Pedro knew that Vimto had by then revoked the power, or become bankrupt or insane or had died.

Pedro later sells to Quentin. Quentin can conclusively presume that Pedro did not know of any revocation, provided that the power came into effect in the 12 months preceding 1 October 1989. Quentin will *not* raise any requisition as to Pedro's knowledge. He will simply compare the date of the power and the date of the conveyance. If the 1989 conveyance was executed by Alexis more than 12 months after the date of the power, Pedro will be asked to make the statutory declaration.

Again, the requisition to Pedro is not 'did you know of any revocation?' but is 'supply the statutory declaration'. Pedro may be lying in his teeth when he makes the declaration, but the title he gives to Quentin will be sound.

(g) A Power of Attorney Delegating a Trust

Section 25 of the Trustee Act 1925 (as amended by s.9 of the Powers of Attorney Act 1971) provides that a trustee (including a trustee for sale) can by a power of attorney delegate the exercise of his trust and powers for up to 12 months.

The power of attorney must be executed in the presence of a witness, and notice of it must be given to the other trustees.

A trustee cannot delegate to his fellow-trustee if there are only the two of them. One of three or more trustees can delegate to a fellow-trustee. Nor can a trustee use the statutory form of power of attorney under s.10 of the Powers of Attorney Act 1971 even if the trustee is also a beneficial owner (see *Walia* v. *Michael Naughton Ltd* [1985]).*

So if A and B own the legal estate on trust for sale for themselves as beneficial co-owners:

(i) A cannot appoint B as his attorney;
(ii) If A appoints X as his attorney, the power must comply with the Trustee Act 1925, otherwise it will be void.

N.B. At the time of writing, the Trustee Delegation Bill is before Parliament. If enacted, it will, among other things, provide a statutory form of power of attorney to be used by a trustee. It will also distinguish between trustees who hold in trust for others, and who will have to comply with restrictions when delegating the trust, and trustees who hold in trust only for themselves, who will not.

(h)   The Application of these Rules to Registered Title

Although this chapter is on the subject of unregistered title, this is a convenient time to consider the application of these rules to a registered title.

A transfer by the attorney of the registered proprietor will again be valid, provided that the person dealing with the attorney did not know of the revocation of the power. The transferee will then apply for registration of the transfer. It is now the *Registrar* who is concerned as to whether the transferee did or did not know of any revocation. Therefore, if the transfer did not take place within 12 months of the power, the Registrar will require the transferee to provide the Registrar with a statutory declaration that at the time of completion the transferee did not know of the revocation of the power. If the power is a security power, the transferee must declare that he did not know that the power was not in fact given by way of security, and did not know of any revocation with the attorney's consent. The power, or a certified copy of it, must also be filed (Rule 82 of Land Registration Rules 1925, as substituted by Land Registration (Powers of Attorney) Rules 1986).

This declaration must also accompany an application for first registration.

(i)   The Enduring Powers of Attorney Act 1985

The purpose of this Act is to enable a principal to appoint an attorney whose authority will not be revoked by the principal becoming mentally incapable. The power must be created while the principal is of sound mind, and so long as he remains mentally capable the power operates as an ordinary power of attorney. It may confer a general authority on the attorney, or empower him to do only those things specified by the power. An enduring power is effective from the moment it is executed, so the attorney is empowered to dispose of the principal's property even while the principal is still mentally capable. It can be made clear in the power that it is only to become effective when the principal becomes mentally incapable if this precaution is felt to be necessary. The power must be in a prescribed form (see the Enduring Powers of Attorney (Prescribed Form) Regulations 1990 SI No. 1376). It must, for example, contain an express statement that the principal intends the power to continue notwithstanding any later mental incapacity, and the principal must confirm that he has read this statement. The power must be executed by the principal and the attorney in the presence of a witness.

When the donor becomes mentally incapable, the attorney is under a statutory duty to register the power with the court, and his authority to deal with the principal's property is suspended until the power is registered. Once the power is registered, the principal cannot revoke the power unless he recovers mental capacity *and* the court confirms the revocation. The power, although not revoked by the mental incapacity of the principal, is revoked by his death or bankruptcy.

The risk for the person dealing with the attorney is not so much the risk of *revocation* of the power, as of its invalidity, or its suspension through non-registration. The Act contains provisions to protect the person dealing with the attorney against such possibilities. The protection depends on the ignorance of these matters. Subsequent purchasers have the benefit of a conclusive presumption that the transaction between the attorney and the person dealing with him is valid if either it took place within one year of the power being registered, or the person dealing with the attorney makes a statutory declaration that he had no reason to doubt the existence of the attorney's authority to enter into the transaction.

As an exception to the rule set out in (g), a power under the 1985 Act will delegate any powers which the principal had as a trustee, even though the attorney is the sole fellow-trustee. So, if A and B were co-owners of land, a power given by A to B under the 1985 Act would enable B to sell the property effectively on his own (although in the name of A and B) and by himself to give a good receipt for the purchase price (s.3(3) of the Enduring Powers of Attorney Act 1985).

This is one reason why a power of attorney is often drawn up as an enduring power rather than an ordinary one. A second reason is that a delegation of a trust under s.25 Trustee Act 1925 lasts for only 12 months. A delegation of a trust under the 1985 Act lasts indefinitely. A third reason is that the presumption as to the validity of the transaction is applied to any dealing within 12 months of the registration of the power rather than of its execution. So no statutory declaration is needed even though the power may have been executed more than 12 months before the attorney executes the conveyance.

N.B. Clauses in the Trustee Delegation Bill (mentioned above) may prevent this circumvention of the usual rule that proceeds of sale have to be paid to at least two trustees.

9.6 Clearing a Mortgage off the Title

In unregistered title, there are three usual ways of removing a mortgage from the title.

(a) Redemption

The purchaser is entitled to evidence that the mortgage loan has been repaid. Section 115 of the Law of Property Act 1925 provides that a receipt for all the money due under the mortgage endorsed on the mortgage and executed by the lender will discharge the mortgaged property from all interest and principal secured by the mortgage. The section also provides that the receipt should name the person making the payment. When investigat-

ing the discharge of the mortgage, you need to check that the person named
in the receipt as making the payment was the person who then owned the
mortgaged property. If he was, the receipt does discharge the mortgage. If
he was not, the receipt does not discharge the mortgage; instead it transfers ownership of it from the original lender to the person named as making
the payment. This is why care is needed in dating the receipt. Suppose that
Bella owns Blackacre, which is mortgaged to the Northlands Bank. She contracts to sell Blackacre free of the mortgage to Catherine, and the sale is
completed on 6 March. Part of the purchase price is used to pay off the
Bank. The Bank endorses the receipt on the mortgage deed and names
Bella as having made the payment. It is correct to name Bella rather than
Catherine as the arrangement in the agreement for sale was that the mortgage was to be discharged by the seller before Blackacre was conveyed to
Catherine. The receipt must be dated either 6 March or earlier. If it is dated
7 March, Bella is not at that date the owner of the land. The receipt transfers the mortgage from Northlands Bank to Bella. Although in theory Bella
would have taken a transfer of the mortgage, probably nothing would have
to be done to clear the title. If the conveyance to Catherine said that Bella's
title was 'free from incumbrances', Bella would be estopped from asserting
the mortgage (see *Cumberland Court (Brighton) Ltd v. Taylor* [1964]).

A receipt will not operate as a transfer if the receipt provides otherwise.

A building society will use the form of receipt allowed by the Building
Societies Act 1986. This merely acknowledges receipt of the money. It does
not name the person making the payment, and cannot operate as a transfer.

The seller's mortgage   As has already been mentioned, banks and building
societies sometimes refuse to execute the receipt in advance of completion.
The purchaser's solicitor may accept undertakings as discussed in section
7.4(c).

(b)   By Release

On the sale of part of the land in an unregistered title, the lender may
release that part from the mortgage.

(c)   By Overreaching

Ths is discussed in section 7.4(c). A purchaser will not see a receipt on the
mortgage of the mortgagee who is selling, nor on any subsequent mortgage.
In unregistered title, the power of sale is implied into any mortgage by deed
(s.101 of the Law of Property Act 1925).

9.7   Establishing a Title by Adverse Possession

A seller can establish that he has a good title by proving adverse possession. However, he must establish not only that he (and possibly his prede-
cessors) have been in possession of the land, but also that the possession